Transformational Groups

CREATING A NEW
SCORECARD FOR
GROUPS

Transformational Groups

Ed Stetzer +
Eric Geiger

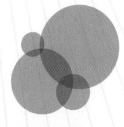

PUBLISHING GROUP
NASHVILLE, TENNESSEE

978-1-4336-8330-5

Published by B&H Publishing Group
Nashville, Tennessee

Dewey Decimal Classification: 269.2
Subject Heading: MINISTRY \ CHURCH GROUP WORK \
EVANGELISTIC WORK

6 7 8 9 10 11 12 • 22 21 20 19 18

This book is dedicated to group leaders who diligently serve each week, leading their groups to love Jesus more deeply and to join Him on His mission to reach the world.

From Ed:

To the Life Group leaders at Grace Church. Your sacrifice and willing spirit encourages and amazes me. Without you, Grace Church would not be possible.

From Eric:

To the couples in our first small group in Miami (the Derringers, Prussners, Riggs, and Lewises): I thought of you while writing this book. Your presence and encouragement shaped Kaye and me.

ACKNOWLEDGMENTS

THERE ARE TOO MANY people to properly thank, and we will inevitably forget someone (or even groups of someones), but we feel indebted to the following people for their contributions to this effort.

The Transformational Group research project and this book would not be possible without the tireless efforts of Scott McConnell, Director of LifeWay Research, and his team including Lizette Beard, Daniel Price, Matt Lowe, and Shirley Cross. Scott is a brilliant researcher and his team is without equal. We cannot imagine a more capable group of people and their diligence and excellence is evident throughout the book. Thank you.

The team at B&H Publishing continues to elicit our gratitude and respect for their extraordinary commitment to what they do. Devin Maddox, Jennifer Lyell, and so many others who have poured their time and energy into this effort. If this book is worth reading, it is in large part due to their efforts. We are incredibly grateful.

Dino Senesi is a friend and pastor and we are grateful for his faithful efforts helping us as we put this book together.

We also would like to thank Micah Fries, Vice President of LifeWay Research. Micah has shepherded this book from beginning to end, and without his energies the book would not be in print.

Finally, and most importantly, our wives and children deserve the lion's share of our gratitude. With hectic travel schedule, busy work calendars, and additional demands that require work even when we are at home, our families' support is absolutely necessary to everything we do, and without it, we would not succeed. We are well loved by our families, and for that we are grateful.

CONTENTS

Introduction

Groups matter—a lot.

In the midst of a thousand discussions—from being missional, to the value of preaching, to how we make better disciples—we can't forget the importance of groups in transformation.

Neither of us is in full-time local church ministry now. We serve the church by providing research and resources. Yet both of us are intimately involved in small-group life because we know groups matter.

I (Ed) serve as lead pastor of a church I planted a couple of years ago. Since my full-time job is president of LifeWay Research, I volunteer as lead pastor of Grace Church. We have a couple of full-time staff and a team of other volunteers.

I can do only a few things as a volunteer lead pastor. I preach and lead the staff—both of those are givens. But then I have to make a choice of what else I can do.

I could counsel, teach more, lead men's ministry, start something new, or a million other different things (many of which a full-time pastor would do). But I have to choose, and I choose leading a Life Group every Sunday night.

You see, I'm convinced that *you can't lead what you do not live*. So I am a pastor, but I am a small-group leader. Actually our group multiplied two weeks ago as of this writing, so I am a multiplying small-group leader. That's why I write this book.

I (Eric) serve alongside Ed as one of the vice presidents of LifeWay, where I lead the Church Resources Division. I also am honored to serve as teaching pastor in a local church in the Nashville area. Before we moved here, my wife and I were involved in small groups for young couples for many years in Miami. Those in our small group there are still dear friends and people the Lord used as sanctifying encouragers in our lives.

Since we are no longer considered a young couple and could not be a part of the small group as members, we now lead a young couples' group at our church in Nashville. Some of the couples are so young they call my wife "Mrs. Kaye," which has only heightened our awareness of our approaching "middle-age" status.

Kaye and I love being in a small group. We have seen the Lord use the community He develops in a group environment to mature His people—to mature us. We lead a group not as a job but to invest in the spiritual transformation of others.

So we are small-group leaders and practitioners every week. Our desire is to serve you by helping you see group life lived out more effectively and fruitfully. We share as pastors, researchers, and small-group leaders because we are convinced—and we think that you should be convinced—that small-group life matters. Church leader, your groups matter.

In a world that is pushing against community, the church must push for authentic community. We have to work to keep the values of the world out of the church body. The fact is that the world's values are not the values of the people of God.

Yet we often forget that this includes community. The world pushes us to isolation and then offers superficial interaction as a false community. Part of what the church of God (as the people of God) must do is to show a better way. It's the biblical way of community.

So we share our hearts for community.

This book is a result of decades of pastoral leadership, countless small groups, and multiple research projects from the last three years. Our primary research sources come from three projects: the Transformational Discipleship project, the Transformational Groups project, and continuing research on group leaders. May it lead you to care about community enough that you take the necessary steps to help make small-group community a reality at your church. We also pray that it will help your groups make more and deeper disciples.

1
Transformational Group Manifesto

LeaderSpeak

> *Sin demands to have a man by himself.*
> *It withdraws him from the community. The more*
> *isolated a person is, the more destructive will*
> *be the power of sin over him.*
> —Dietrich Bonhoeffer

First Step: *Create an intentional group DNA.*

Were you to ever venture just north of San Francisco into Muir Woods, an incredible forest of sequoia trees, you would no doubt be provoked to a sense of awe over the strength and endurance of the massive trees. Sequoias are sometimes referred to as the largest living things on earth, reaching almost 250 feet in the air and standing for as many as fifteen hundred years.

When you stand before their enormous trunks and beneath a canopy more than twenty stories above you, it's hard not to feel tiny and envious at the same time. If you could have a conversation with one (not that either of us have attempted that), would you not want to ask, "How? How have you done it? How have you stood strong through all the storms of life, all the difficult situations? How have you not toppled?"

Their response may be surprising.

You would probably assume that deep roots would be the fundamental reason the sequoias around you could date back to a few decades from the collapse of the Roman Empire. That is not the case at all, however, as each tree's roots grow only about four feet in the ground. While going deeper helps many trees remain upright, the sequoia you stand before like an ant has not overcome the difficulties of life because of its depth.

The answer doesn't lie down below in the earth but all around the tree. If you looked around, you would notice that sequoia trees grow only in groves. While their roots go only about four feet deep into the ground, their roots intermingle with the other sequoias next to them. One tree has other trees surrounding it, supporting it and keeping it strong. Each tree stands strong through the centuries because each tree has an interdependent posture.

No sequoia grows alone.

The connection to our spiritual walk should be obvious—no believer is transformed alone. Just as the mighty sequoia would topple without a community of supporting trees, believers who seek transformation apart from a Christian community are vulnerable to spiritually topple in the winds of adversity.

In many circles, believers are reclaiming "personal spiritual disciplines" that help them encounter the grace of God. Moreover, the plethora of resources provided to Christians for "personal spiritual growth" is constantly on the rise, while simultaneously some church leaders are experimenting with "personal spiritual growth plans" for members, customized to the individual's learning style and current assessment of his spiritual life.

While we are grateful for the encouragement, resources, and opportunities for individuals to grow, we fear that the beauty and necessity of community may be lost in the forest of resources for the individual. If community is ignored, the resources may fill minds while not transforming hearts.

How important is community for the body of Christ? Is it just a detail many people can live without? Is community an option when you dream about your church design? Or is community one of those annoying consumer needs you have to provide?

Transformation is a communal experience, not an individual exercise. Jesus, God on earth, understood this fact. His model of disciple making must be ours. Jesus chose twelve, a small group. The synergy that occurred in that group of twelve aided greatly in the process of making these men mature disciples. The conversations they engaged in, the times they served Rabbi Jesus together, the processing of Jesus' teachings around a campfire, even the missteps these men shared were all in Jesus' plan for making them into the mature disciples He needed them to be. Doing life together is an unquestionable essential in the disciple-making process.

When we speak of the value of community, we are not speaking of arguing about the right kind of small group. None of the "groups" discussion will matter until we all see this as a greater subject than groups. No matter how you define *groups*—Life Groups, Sunday school, discipleship classes, or Bible fellowships—the importance is the same. Church leaders—including pastoral staff, elders, deacons, and leadership teams—must see community as a biblical nonnegotiable, an essential for transformation, a necessity for building lives that stand the test of time.

This brings us to the Transformational Groups project.

Transformational Groups

As we looked across the church world, we recognized a discipleship deficit. In a previous research project, the Transformational Discipleship project, this was confirmed in profound ways. Through our research, personal experience, and understanding of Scripture, we also firmly believe that Christian maturity happens most effectively in smaller groups of people.

In light of this, we wondered if we could use research to determine exactly what core characteristics are present in each group that is effectively creating transformed disciples. Regardless of the form of your group, what are the necessary components that consistently rise to the surface as integral to the disciple-making process? Through all of this, we thought this research might be helpful to churches as they seek to be more effective at leading people to become fully transformed followers of Jesus.

Your church, no matter how together it looks on the surface, will never become all that God wants if community is just an annoying detail, just something else to place on the calendar. The pastor(s) and church leaders must believe deeply in and declare the importance of community to Sunday morning consumers who prefer comfort to community. Maybe we have spent too much time inviting people to groups and not enough time declaring truth and expecting group participation.

That seemed to be the case when we looked at the research. Immediately we noticed three disappointing findings that paint a sad picture of Christian community. It further bolstered in our mind the need to more boldly declare the necessity of community, of sequoia-tree Christianity.

Disappointment 1. Disorganized Discipleship

Our first disappointment was that over half of pastors surveyed said they have *no visible strategy for their group life.*

As an indication of that, we asked an additional question: Who is responsible for selecting the curriculum for small groups? Two-thirds of the pastors reported they let the group leaders decide. The "study what you want" approach is irresponsible unless there is clear training that equips group leaders for wise choices. Without that, the haphazard approach can be a bit terrifying. This greatly inhibits the church developing a consistent culture for how groups are going to function and mature over time. It works against a common direction and vision and creates a mismatched, helter-skelter kind of chaotic ethos within the church.

Imagine if pastors and church leaders put as much energy into their worship service as they do their group ministry. Just let Bob, the worship leader, pick whatever random song he likes. It could be one from a hymnal, a song he heard on the radio driving to church that morning, or a hit from when he was a teenager. The musicians and choir could follow his lead or go do their own thing. The ushers could stroll down the aisle to collect the offering whenever the urge struck. This type of environment would be chaos, off-putting to any guest that came through and distracting for a member trying to participate and worship God with other believers. In short, it would not be something most pastors and church leaders would allow for very long. Yet, according to the research, groups are often handled in this way.

Small groups should receive similar care and attention as the worship service. A church member may casually know the people they sit beside during the sermon, but if community is emphasized and practiced, they will intimately know and love the people beside them in their small group. But this does not happen overnight or without effort. Groups require constant attention to be transformational.

Everyone seems to be talking about having groups, and everyone seems to want them. But sometimes they get frustrating and messy because they involve placing sinners in close proximity to one another. When these problems arise, even though they should be expected, there is a drag on the group conversation. Churches come to realize groups can be hard to manage and hard to start, so they can give up too quickly. They think they've tried groups, but they haven't given them time. Then another book comes out promising great results, and the pastor jumps to something different, as if it will be the answer to every small-group problem. Remember: *there is never a one-time, final group solution for everything.* There is, however, a constant cycle of learning, trying, and changing. Transformation takes time, patience, endurance, organization, and unified direction.

Concluding and sticking to a group strategy that is right for your church and culture for a significant period of time is the only way an effective, transformational group ministry can be established. We have a friend who serves as the groups pastor for a large church in the central United States. Over the last four years he has been asked by the senior pastor he serves alongside to revisit the church's group strategy at least four times. Each time my friend has researched the new ideology, trained leaders in the new way of doing groups, and then begun the hard work of implementing the new principles and practices into all of the church's groups. Many of his group leaders have bailed, and most of those who are left are discouraged. Group members who were once excited about being in a group are no longer in a group or are reconsidering being in a group, and some people have left the church.

In order to overcome disappointment, it is essential that church leaders conclude what is the best strategy for doing groups in their context and wholeheartedly embrace that ideology with its principles and practices.

We hope that, before you finish this book, you will have realized the essentials to healthy group life and are well on your way to concluding a groups model that embraces those essentials and is effective in your setting.

Disappointment 2. Comfort and Not Correction

Our second disappointment was that group attenders were primarily looking for comfort from groups more than accountability and correction.

Realistically none of us are going to say we love the accountability part. Neither do we look forward to being corrected through the study of God's Word and the "caring concern" of our brothers or sisters in Christ. But we know the reality of being a Christ follower. We grow best when, in community, we experience both biblical correction and accountability.

People who do not attend groups consider life change in others and correction as the two LEAST important outcomes of a group. Another discovery is that people who are currently not attending groups would prefer a group that meets at the church for only an hour. Obviously they are not interested in making any significant commitment to community. Of these who are NOT attending, 71 percent say they are open to attending, and another 8 percent say they are actively looking for a group.

The gap is quite compelling between what is experienced or wanted and what might actually be needed. Among those who attend a group, the top two outcomes they want are Encouragement and Acceptance. The two outcomes they least desire were Accountability and Correction. Compare that with nonattenders. Their top two desired outcomes are Encouragement and Support, and their two least desired outcomes were Life-Change in Others and Correction.

People may see these numbers and come to varying conclusions, but to us they indicate a discipleship deficit. Even those committed to group attendance don't seem to be experiencing a high level of accountability and correction. The purpose of accountability in community is to lead others to repentance in everyday life through biblical correction with grace, knowing that every sin is unbelief in the gospel. Group DNA should include a culture of accountability and practice biblical correction.

Spiritual growth begins with discomfort. When God's Word points out a seemingly outlandish expectation, this creates internal discomfort. When the Holy Spirit whispers a seemingly unreasonable expectation, discomfort is the outcome. The idea that spiritual growth begins with discomfort is a fact many church members and church leaders have been unwilling or unable to embrace. In fact, because we often find ourselves in the mode of longing to grow a church numerically rather than growing individuals in the church spiritually, we will be tempted to downplay the biblical expectations of a disciple so that attenders will be comfortable and choose to become church members. If we're going to work in tandem with

Jesus in the disciple-making process, we must be willing to allow His standard to be the standard for each of His disciples, and we must hold one another accountable to live out those standards in a safe, healthy, committed group.

Disappointment 3. Personal Priority

Our third disappointment was that group attenders and nonattenders seemed to be looking for their own needs first.

We don't want to disrespect people who are interested in things like "following Christ more closely" as the most desirable outcome of their group. That is the "right answer" from our perspective. But clearly when given four choices, both attenders and nonattenders rank the four categories in the same order. Their focus seemed to be inward first, then outward.

Ranking Group Outcomes

Outcome	Attendees	Nonattenders
Following Christ More Closely	56%	42%
Growing Closer to One Another	19%	24%
New People Hearing the Gospel	18%	19%
Serving People Outside the Church	9%	15%

Groups must prioritize the Great Commission (go and make disciples) and the Great Commandment (love God and love your neighbor as yourself). The benefit will be to the participant, the recipient of love and good news, and for the glory of God. Serving people outside the church and having new people hear the gospel should be a DNA issue. We understand, however, that some groups are for the express purpose of teaching or formation, such as Sunday school and other courses taught in the church. Groups that meet in homes are not necessarily neighborhood focused or evangelistic in nature either.

We believe the culture in both situations should be reconsidered. No matter the context, groups should have an outward-focused, an evangelistic DNA. But we are all naturally self-centered and have been since birth. Placing the needs of others ahead of our own will not happen without intentionality in pastoral leadership as well as group leaders.

Wave the Community Banner with Passion

Think about this scenario. What if your local Walmart store strategically positioned representatives from their paint department by the checkout lanes? And these paint reps' job all day would be to examine what was in the shopping carts of everyone checking out. If you had anything from the paint department, you would be fine. But in case you didn't have any paint or supplies, look out, there would be trouble.

An ugly and embarrassing scene of interrogation would transpire. You would hear about not caring for the inside and outside of where you lived, even if you were renting. You would be insulted and directed back to the paint section to make up for how lazy and cheap you were.

This is an absurd situation that would never happen, right? Why? *Because you are a customer, and it's your business what you buy.* Not to mention, demanding customers to buy something they don't want is really bad for business.

Did you ever think people who attend your church are comfortable without community because you are making it comfortable for them? We aren't suggesting you insult people by calling them lazy or cheap for not being in community. But if you went to the hypothetical Walmart, you would leave knowing at least one thing—they value paint. The most important distinction, however, is that the people in your church are not customers, and you aren't called to make customers of all nations.

A pastor can tell if the focus is transformation based on how groups are promoted. You see, people will gather in groups to become what the pastor espouses. For instance, if a pastor says to the congregation, "Many of you are new to our church. You've mentioned to me that you need to make friends. That's what our groups are for. If you want to make friends, join a group."

This pastor's congregation is now going to be involved in a group so that they can find, make, and have friendships. What happens in a group at this church will be quite different from what occurs in a church where the pastor announces, "It is our goal for every person in this church to become a mature disciple of Jesus Christ. This happens when you are in a group with other growing disciples where you are learning the Bible together, holding one another accountable to spend time with God daily, and living a lifestyle that looks more and more like the lifestyle of Jesus."

Believing in community and establishing transformational communities is not the same thing.

You are to make disciples, and that cannot happen apart from community. The two are inseparable, and this must be communicated clearly and consistently by leadership. If you wonder why the people lack any sense of investment in community, it may be because the leaders lack it as well. When the pastor sends the wrong message, you should not be surprised when it results in the wrong outcome.

The pastor may do the fall and spring promotion of your classes or groups in a rote manner or perhaps sit by passively as discipleship and education leaders make their pleas. An occasional slide, video clip, or spot in your Sunday morning brochure about groups or classes may even appear periodically. But do we really believe community is a mandate for true spiritual growth and Christ formation in people?

If we listened to your sermons and followed you around for a year, what would convince us that you are all about biblical community? What would prove that you believe community is of supernatural and eternal importance to the mission of God, for the glory of God?

We can see how much God values it because community is evident through the biblical narrative, from Genesis to Revelation. We can see it is biblical and critical.

God said, "It is not good for the man to be alone" (Gen. 2:18). But sin destroyed the perfect community in the garden. Then God established a new community in Israel to bless the nations. But this new community was far from perfect. Eventually Jesus came and started an even better community, though not yet perfect, with the establishment of the local church—the "called out ones." Then in Revelation, community is fully restored. We're all together in perfect community for eternity.

We see what a perfect community looks like throughout Scripture, by seeing how God Himself exists in Trinity. Genesis 1:26, "Let *Us* make man in *Our* image." Or in Isaiah 6, "Who should *I* send? Who will go for *Us*?" (v. 8). God has always existed in community. Out of this reality, this truth of eternal and perfect community, came the declaration: "it is not good for the man to be alone." The three persons of the trinitarian God are in community with one another, with distinct functions and relationships. As image bearers of God, we reflect this trinitarian community as we live in true community with others.

Growth Happens through Community

Scripture constantly paints the picture for us that growth happens in community, and there we see the eternal value. Growth happens in community because the Bible places community as a critical step of obedience for the Christ follower. So the Christ follower outside of community is living in disobedience. Community is assumed—if I am out of community, I am out of God's will. The church (*ecclesia*) is the gathering of the called-out ones. They are called out of darkness, out of hiding and shame (Gen. 3:8–10) and into relationship with God and with others through Jesus. As related believers we are no longer unknown, independent people who are disassociated with one another and with God. Rather we are neighbors with other believers, and we are rightfully members of the household of God. This house is built on the foundation of the apostles and prophets, Christ Jesus Himself being the cornerstone (see Eph. 2:19–20). As with the sequoia trees, no believer is transformed alone.

Our roots gain their true strength because God is in community with us. If it were just "us," there would be human synergy. Positive results can flow from merely human relationships and people's desire to collaborate. But biblical community is different from what happens at your homeowners association. Life-investing relationships within the church body carry more significance than the local PTA.

Because biblical community involves a supernatural God component, it becomes a nonnegotiable in our local churches. We need to stop presenting community as just another option for the religious consumer and start presenting it as God's will for everyone. It should be seen as the reality of those within the church and the refuge for those without.

The world is looking for community, and you can tell it even when you observe those who are often the most hostile to God. Atheists have started to form what amounts to churches without God (with CNN recently reporting about atheist "congregations"). Some gather weekly for music and a message. Despite their rejection of God, they cannot help but see the value in one of His gifts to us— community. How ironic that while atheists are beginning to recognize the worth of merely being together as humans, many Christians are dismissing the significance of a supernatural community.

When a guy is struggling with loving his wife, it's going to take a community of guys around him to help him love her as Christ loved the church (Eph. 5:25). Or when he is struggling with an addiction to alcohol or pornography, he needs to experience grace coupled with truth (John 1:14, 17).

When a single mother is struggling with sexual purity, she needs people around her who can love and understand her as well as keep her accountable to biblical principles. Or when she's wrestling with the soul-crushing news that her only child has a serious medical issue, what's going to hold her strong? Often it is the sequoia trees surrounding her.

A friend once found himself in a very difficult emotional place. In fact, although he is a pastor, he was diagnosed with depression, a debilitating darkness that might have taken him out of ministry if it hadn't been for a community of friends that carried the day for him. A bit of his story . . . this pastor was a bivocational church planter with a struggling but healthy church plant. Four years of double duty had kept him from taking care of himself physically as well as emotionally. As his positive personality became nonexistent, his wife suggested he see a counselor. It was here the diagnosis was declared. The counselor, being a good friend of his and having been part of the group ministry at the pastor's church, asked him if he would allow his group to know his situation and journey with him through it until the light of God's light was evident to him again. He agreed. And in time the darkness lifted, and his heart was alive once again.

Had my friend done as so many before him have done, he would probably be another statistic, another pastor having divorced the wife God so graciously placed in his life, being involved in an unnecessary affair, having committed suicide, or exiting the ministry. But there were some intertwining roots that held him up when he couldn't stand alone.

We live in a society that is obsessed with autonomous individualism, the idea that all I need is myself and I can make it on my own. This lie keeps people from connecting to one another and is slowly killing their souls. Many of the most influential sins of our culture— pornography, greed, failure to take responsibility—are fostered in the context of radical individualism. If we listen, we can hear the echo of Genesis. "It is not good for the man to be alone." God didn't design people to live outside of community.

The gospel gives us a countercultural opportunity. For years the church has sought to be relevant and engage culture. But now we have an opportunity to be a culturally-relevant counterculture. The counterculture is this: *we don't buy into autonomous individualism.* Through Christ the church really is a family and a body.

The health, long-term mission, and viability of the church are not going to be determined by those who gather on Sunday morning. The future of the church will be determined by the depth of its disciples. People in communities through small groups or classes beyond Sunday morning are our future. They are our future because in these settings mature, countercultural disciples are made.

We End Up in Eternal Community

The last book in the Bible is placed there for a reason—it tells us how this is all going to end. We get a snapshot of the future, one of which we should constantly remind ourselves. We need to store it on our proverbial computers and phones and tape it on our refrigerators so we see it every morning. We should never forget—we all end up in community with God for eternity:

> Then I heard a loud voice from the throne: Look! God's dwelling is with humanity, and He will live with them. They will be His people, and God Himself will be with them and be their God. He will wipe away every tear from their eyes. Death will no longer exist; grief, crying, and pain will exist no longer, because the previous things have passed away. (Rev. 21:3–4)

Did you catch that? God's eternal dwelling is with "humanity" (as in men and women) not man; "them" not me; and "people" not a person. We end up in eternal community dwelling with God and with all of humankind.

How incredible will that be? Although you can argue that gathering will be large, you are missing the point. In that day we will all be able to relate perfectly to one another and to God. The size of the gathering only reveals you are not alone.

We will be in community with God and one another in heaven. Our rooms or mansions will not be the size of an airplane bathroom, and we will never again go bowling alone. God's "dwelling" is the word also translated "tabernacle," saying that God will literally "pitch a tent" over "us." That will be a place of safety and security we have never known before. We will forever be transformed from a "me" to an "us" in community with God.

Eternal community with God and one another will be sweet. Everything that sabotaged our efforts to be in community on earth will become a "previous" thing. Our baggage—our struggles to love, trust, and relate—will "have passed away."

How important is biblical community together on earth? As important as it will be in heaven. Biblical community is where I can love and be loved, where I can receive grace and extend grace, where I can watch transformation in the lives of my friends and experience my own transformation, where other sequoias can hold me up and where I can intertwine my roots with others, and where I can experience God's glory in this life and in the life to come like never before.

Yet the "church" often becomes some nebulous entity that becomes our life force versus community. This entity is often reduced to "all about me," my preferences and my needs. The local church now is God in community with us. A smaller group or class is the same thing—God in community with us. Because of this fact, community is vital to our survival and growth. Community is of eternal value and community is eternal. In community we become more like Jesus as we "accept one another, just as the Messiah also accepted you, to the glory of God" (Rom. 15:7).

Think about it—community is how God is and is how He transforms us into His likeness. It has been so since the beginning of time. God chose to be community as Father, Son, and Holy Spirit. He then established His Old Testament community, the children of Israel. Jesus then birthed the church, a community of believers who are a family. And as weird as it seems to some people, Jesus isn't coming back to get each of us, individuals, He's returning for a community, His church. We were designed for and are to live and grow in community.

Nailing Your Convictions to the Door

There comes a point in the groups-building phase where you declare the distinctions of your project. You must instill your convictions instilled into the DNA of groups and nail your motives to the door for all to see.

Martin Luther, a German monk from the early sixteenth century, was famous for nailing his convictions in view of the public. His "Ninety-Five Theses" was a document containing the summary of his perceived errors of faith and practice in the church. He nailed them to the door of Castle Church in Wittenberg, Germany. To no one's surprise Luther was kicked out of the church. But his declaration of salvation through Christ alone, and the Bible as the standard for Christian faith and conduct, ignited what we know as the Protestant Reformation.

Other people have sparked great social movements by their passionate declarations of belief. Martin Luther King's "I Have a Dream" and John F. Kennedy's "Man on the Moon" speeches are famous public declarations that influenced generations of people. Some consider these people radical, others troublemakers. But they are people with strong passion and belief. And belief inspires people, but that belief has to carry with it a call to action and commitment.

Manifesto is an Italian word that means "clear." While it has been used negatively and positively throughout history, it is simply a declaration of belief and intentions. A manifesto reveals beliefs that drive actions. Your groups need clear focus on the biblical underpinnings for community. Groups of people in community can no longer be an option for your church. It is a biblical fact, not a passing fad. We believe there is a discipleship deficit in the local church that must be declared and acted upon.

Although Christians often overuse the cliché "change the world," here we sadly use it as a negative. Our discipleship deficit has changed the world but not for the better. We are responsible for the fact that what God wants is not happening, particularly in America. Simply put, Christians are not following Christ, and we are making no difference in our neighborhoods, much less the world.

A call to discipleship and spiritual maturity is a call to biblical community. The call to discipleship is an invitation to hear and obey the voice of God. Also, a call to discipleship is a call to follow Jesus and be sent as a missionary to your community and world.

We believe it is important to establish the beliefs that drive your behaviors as leaders. The exercise will be valuable and help you create a transformational culture.

Many churches design and build their facilities so groups will have comfortable places to meet in a convenient location. More specifically they contract a designer for the facility. Then they entertain bids from construction companies to do the building. And finally they choose the best company for the job. The details are excruciating, but each one is critical to the success of the building. Designing, bidding, and building a building aren't parts of an organic process but a highly intentional process. Groups need to be designed, considered carefully, and built with wise intentionality.

The design and build phases of groups and classes rarely get the attention needed to create transformational environments. Doing groups without a clear statement of convictions makes community a preference instead of a conviction.

The energy and intentionality needed for building group environments for transformation is usually invested elsewhere—namely Sunday mornings. Groups often get whatever energy, staff, and budget are leftover. With the abundance of relatively inexpensive "plug-and-play" materials, it seems simple. Find a willing leader, provide quality materials, saturate church communication streams with advertising, and the group happens, all by itself.

Yet, groups and classes can be missed opportunities if they merely exist. Everything on the surface may look right. Leaders, space, and materials along with eager disciples populating classrooms or living rooms give the appearance that transformation is not far behind. But transformational group culture does not happen all by itself with just the right teaching material. It is not a boxed cake mix that just needs water. It is a recipe, a process that requires intentionality and care.

Finding the right leaders is the first step in creating a transformational culture in groups. But the building process does not stop there. Deciding what your groups are going to value is another critical step. The core convictions of your group are vital because character gives definition and structure to what is happening. The character of your group is also central to determining the outcome of your group.

Find the Right Beliefs

Leaders influence people mostly by what they believe. Beliefs will lead to passionate discussions, but most importantly beliefs lead to radical actions. So why do we talk about beliefs at this part of the building phase? Because beliefs are powerful and inspirational. Beliefs unify people around vision and purpose.

So here is a sample of a Transformational Group Manifesto. Use this as a guide, but ultimately we believe you should create your own. You cannot possibly list every important doctrine in the Bible, so don't confuse this list with a doctrinal statement. Your church should already have a list somewhere anyway. These core convictions drive the way you do groups on a weekly basis. When you write your own, you will have similarities but also unique Scripture, expressions, and elements.

1. *The Bible.* Because we believe the Bible is God's love in writing, we pursue its truth as the center of all we do. We will pursue studying the Bible as the focal point of our weekly meetings.

The only specific picture of what actually happened in smaller groups in the Bible is in Acts 2:42–47. We know that early Christians met in homes constantly, and they also gathered in temples when possible.

Here's one window into biblically-based, small group activities: "And they devoted themselves to the apostles' teaching, to the fellowship, to the breaking of bread, and to the prayers" (Acts 2:42). We will talk more about behaviors and activities in chapter 6, but for our purposes now notice that they were "devoted."

The people in the early church were truly creatures of the Word. The "apostles' teaching" was worthy of their devotion. The complete Scripture as we have it was not in their hands, but they did have Scripture to study. Peter preached from the words of the prophet Joel at Pentecost as well as the psalms of David. The people who made up the early church were truly creatures of the Word.

Healthy groups study the Word. One of the reasons we gather is to study. But study is different from lecture. Their devotion evolved from their full engagement of study and learning.

My (Ed) wife had some correction for me recently about the way I was leading my group. I lead a group, or Life Group as we call it at Grace Church. We were studying *The Gospel Project* at the time. She told me I was doing too much lecturing and not engaging my group in study. Healthy groups "study the Word" together instead of being told what to think.

As a pastor, I'm accustomed to monologue teaching. I prepare for Sunday mornings, and when I preach, no one talks back to me (for the most part). They listen; I talk. People are more devoted when they are discussing instead of only listening. Groups should not be a monologue or even a dialogue. A dialogue is when three people dominate the discussion with the person leading the group while the other eight stare at their Bibles. Group discussion involves listening, waiting, learning together, and shepherding the group to understand the author's original context and the applications that flow from it.

The need for group study does not ignore the fact that not all opinions are created equal. You don't want to pool your collective ignorance in your group by asking everyone in the circle, *What does this passage mean to you?* When we ask that question, we are advocating something we don't want in our groups: *The way to read the Bible is to decide whatever you think it means—because what you think it means, it means.* A conversational Bible study can easily become a night of shared ignorance, and a night of shared ignorance is ultimately a night of false teaching. Rick Howerton, discipleship and small-groups consultant at LifeWay, often tells small-group leaders in his training seminars that "during a conversational Bible study a lot of ideas can circle the runway, but it is the responsibility of the group leader to be certain biblical truth lands."

We use a bridge illustration to help our leaders understand how to teach the Bible:

1. The original Bible *context* is the first side of the bridge (hearers, situation, etc.).
2. The bridge is the *principle or truth* that is universal in the passage.
3. The other side of the bridge is *application*. (Here is where real, open-ended questions can be asked.)

THE BIBLE STUDY BRIDGE

CONTEXT
What does it say?

APPLICATION
What do we do?

A small-group or class Bible study should be a "groupalogue." A groupalogue is a study built on great questions and engaging everyone in the room. You want everyone there to talk to someone. Your effectiveness goes up incredibly as does learning when everyone is talking at the same time. How do you do that without creating chaos? You have people in the group talk to one another. Although questions are being asked your entire time, the most open-ended questions occur during the application time. Discipleship coaching belongs here because everyone will not apply the Scripture in exactly the same ways. But everyone must be challenged to do something as a result of what they heard.

There are multiple ways to be certain application is discussed. These are a few options:

1. Ask everyone in the room, "Now that you've heard what you've heard, what is your next step for God?"
2. "Is there a truth that was established tonight that you're going to continue to wrestle with until it takes hold in your heart?"
3. "Did something God told you through this study tonight unearth a commitment you need to make and be held accountable to? If so, what is that commitment?"
4. "What is the one thing you now know you're supposed to do before we meet again?"

THE GROUPALOGUE

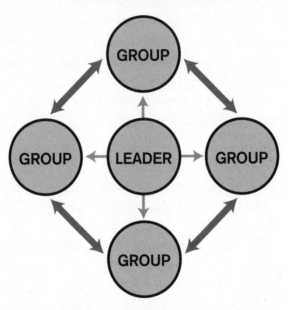

- How much do you talk? (monologue)
- How much do they talk to you? (dialogue)
- How much do they talk to one another? (groupalogue)
- How do the conversations flow during group Bible study?

If we value the Bible and embrace Scripture fully, then the way we teach it is important and intentional. We care about how each of our group leaders teaches God's Word. We care about *The Bridge* and fully engaging in groupalogues. And we care how much time is spent in the discipline of Scripture.

Measure your convictions, not on how well you can articulate or defend them; rather measure your convictions about groups by how they influence behavior.

2. Gospel. Because we believe the gospel is the power of God for salvation to anyone who believes, we pursue gospel conversations with people far from God. Because we believe the gospel is eternal, we will rest in the gospel of grace and pursue gospel conversations with those we disciple.

"The beginning of the *gospel* of Jesus Christ, the Son of God" (Mark 1:1). In the past, the gospel has been reduced to something we "share." We use it to influence people to pray the "sinner's prayer" and become one of us. But the gospel is not the finish line; it's the starting line for life with Christ.

The gospel is worth defining and here's a definition we are using:

> The gospel is the good news that God, who is more holy
> than we can imagine, looked upon with compassion people
> who are more sinful than we would possibly admit and sent
> Jesus into history to establish His kingdom and reconcile
> people and the world to Himself. Jesus, whose love is more
> extravagant than we can measure, came to sacrificially die
> for us so that, by His death and resurrection, we might
> gain through His grace what the Bible defines as new and
> eternal life.

We are not infatuated by the word *gospel*. Neither do we want "gospel" to become the new code language for anything we want it to mean. But the word is used seventy-eight times in the HCSB translation. Paul himself used the word sixty-four times—so we see the gospel not as merely a "big deal" but the "whole deal." The gospel was eternally embedded in Paul's spiritual journey (as it is in ours). His identity was in the gospel of grace; thus, the gospel was his life story:

> But I count my life of no value to myself, so that I may
> finish my course and the ministry I received from the Lord
> Jesus, to testify to the gospel of God's grace. (Acts 20:24)

The word *gospel* has made a big comeback into the Christian vocabulary and an important one. But it's critical that the term is not overused but rather is used to teach and apply the gospel to our lives. New biblical conversations about convictions, doctrine, and what's really important must be a part of group culture. So, when we manifest our intentions, we make groups about more than groups, but we make groups about living in the gospel.

The gospel is much more than a statement of beliefs, but it is part of the entire narrative of God's Word from Genesis to Revelation. Because it is the big story of the Bible delivered in a series of smaller stories of people's lives, then smaller groups become a great place to learn in the gospel:

> Then I saw another angel flying high overhead, having the eternal *gospel* to announce to the inhabitants of the earth— to every nation, tribe, language, and people. (Rev. 14:6)

3. *Mission.* Because we believe in God's mission, we will live "sent" in all places where we find ourselves, looking for opportunities to both show and tell the gospel. We will do small things with great love all over the world for Jesus so that Jesus will be noticed.

Mission is the destiny of every believer who is experiencing life with Jesus. So mission is not a periodic church emphasis or offering. Neither is mission a special Sunday morning when we don't have church in order to serve the community. Mission is much more than that. Hearts that are being changed by God will be supernaturally driven toward His mission.

Jesus spoke of what believers would be able to do after the Holy Spirit came on them (Acts 1:8). Witnessing for Jesus worldwide would be a supernatural result of the Holy Spirit's work. Witnessing or being sent for Jesus would no longer be a "do" but rather a "be," or a supernaturally natural behavior.

As we live in community, we live on mission directed by the Holy Spirit. We will go with Jesus into our communities as harvesters bringing good news: "When He saw the crowds, He felt compassion for them, because they were weary and worn out, like sheep without a shepherd" (Matt. 9:36). We will join Jesus and look for the "weary and worn out."

The end result of community must be mission. If community fails to result in joining Jesus on His mission, then the community is not being formed by the Word and formed in Jesus. The neighborhood in which a group meets should be impacted by the group. In fact, every home where a group meets should be considered another mission point of the church that group represents. The local culture in which a church building is located, one that houses groups, should be impacted by the Christian community that occurs within those groups.

One of my (Eric's) first small groups as an adult was with a group of Christian construction workers. The summer before I went to college, I worked construction in South Louisiana. I was one of the few Christians in the construction company. Duke, Denny, and Gary were three passionate Christ followers who taught me more than I learned in many seminary classrooms. Each of us worked on a different job site, and we would meet together for prayer, Bible study, and lunch in the tool room. Actually everyone else in the construction company called the tool room "the chapel." We were sometimes ridiculed for our faith. Once the tool room was trashed, and "666" was painted all over the walls. But those three men viewed their job sites as a mission field. They were passionate for the people they worked alongside. Each day in the tool room/chapel, they would pray for people they were sharing Christ with on their job site.

Evidently people were watching our little community of Christ followers. Evidently they were watching how we loved one another, cared for one another, and supported one another. A year and a half later, I came home from college and went to an event at a church where I saw Duke. As we hugged, I looked behind him and saw a guy from the scaffolding team, one of the biggest and baddest dudes in the whole crew. Duke said, "Eric, this is our new brother in Christ. He became a Christian a few months ago. We cannot even fit in the chapel anymore because so many guys are getting saved." True community is righteously attractive and evangelistic, or as Jesus stated, "By this all people will know you are My disciples, if you have love for one another" (John 13:35).

4. *Grace.* Because we believe in God's grace, we will live honestly with one another about our shortcomings and withhold judgment when someone talks openly about their struggles.

Groups can become grace communities. But grace is normally more misunderstood than extended or received. A group provides a real-life environment to process grace in a healthy, biblical way.

As with most great truths, our humanity gets in the way of actually embracing and enjoying biblical grace. We struggle between two extremes. The first extreme is to *condemn* bad behavior or to condemn the person who is behaving badly. The Pharisees were really good at condemning. So were those who condemned the woman caught in the act of adultery in John 8. The second extreme is to *condone* bad behavior. Condemn or condone? Neither of these extremes is healthy, biblical, or life giving.

Grace is not as simple as we make it. Those who make it simple tend toward one of those extremes. Grace is a gift from God and others, but it's not an entitlement.

Some who struggle with sin tend to demand grace. Again, we have another contradiction in terms because if grace is a gift, how can you demand it? That would be like pulling a gun on someone to demand a birthday gift.

In the same sense, how can you possibly qualify for grace? Some seem to have an attitude like, "Well, when I think they are really sorry for what they did and also see that they have stopped doing it, then I will extend grace." That is not grace; that is restoration. Restoration is based on your perception of their qualifications. "Have they earned grace?" That makes the contradiction obvious. You can't earn grace any more than you can demand grace.

The key to experiencing grace in community is in the leaders creating a culture of openness. If leaders are more open about their struggles, not only their sins, then people in the group will have permission to be open. What group members see modeled by their leaders is what they will do. This is especially true when it comes to group members unearthing their own failings. What cultivates a culture of double-lives and secrets is fear of rejection. But double-lives are what give people permission to keep on sinning.

Grace and secrets cannot coexist. They are natural enemies.

When my (Eric) wife and I were struggling with the pain of infertility, we wrestled with whom to share our burden with, whom to seek prayer and encouragement from. We opened up to our small group and found deep encouragement and love from our group. They offered grace to us, prayed for us, supported us, and helped pray our kids into existence. We also found that our openness sparked more openness from the others in the group, transparency about their struggles and honesty about their doubts. As groups apply the grace of God to real-life situations, growth occurs.

Will it become awkward at times? Yes! But awkwardness is a sign of progress; it is at that point you know you are bravely going where most groups seldom go. Is a culture of grace dangerous? Yes! But secrets and covering ourselves with fig leaves is more dangerous and really foolish.

If you want group members to be willing to speak of their struggles and sins, every person in the group must first acknowledge that they struggle and sin. Most people, when attending a group meeting, really do believe they may be the only person in the room who has a sin problem. Because of this, they believe they will become the outsider if they tell the group of a struggle or sin they are wrestling with. The fact is, if a circle were drawn on the whiteboard where the group meets and every person who sins was to take their turn to come and write their name in the circle if they sometimes sin, every honest person's name would end up in that circle. While this sounds like some crazy exercise, if a group leader will do this literally or figuratively, it will establish that every person in the group needs grace and will make it much more natural for struggles and even sin to be verbalized and grace to be given and received.

Just as the value of community in the church comes from the pastor, pastoral staff, and key leaders, so does the value of grace. If there is a culture of condemnation in a church, then the leaders are probably not experiencing grace on a deep level, so they will be unable to freely extend it to others.

The Bible is incredibly rich with the message of grace. This message will enable the believer to see the death of their pride and fear. The pastor, in particular, is in desperate need of consistent confession, repentance, and renewal—in other words, the pastor is in desperate need of daily grace.

God's grace molds us into the image of Jesus. So, as we experience grace, extending grace becomes less complicated. Many people in our churches remain in sin because they fear the repercussions of confessing their sin to others. This limits the power of God in their lives. Grace is dangerous, but law is deadly. Let a culture of grace be understood and extended in your groups and classes.

5. *Glory.* Because we believe in God's glory, we will pursue community with one another, practice biblical conflict resolution, and live our lives for His pleasure.

Christians who don't love one another is a contradiction in terms—like gourmet pizza and maple syrup. These oxymorons or contradictions in terms can make us laugh, but as Christ followers we should be embarrassed about the contradictions we live.

God is glorified when Christians are together in loving community, as opposed to His glory being hidden when we are constantly bickering. When we don't do relationships well in the Christian community, we are no different from everyone else. And sadly, there are times where the church is *worse* than everyone else.

Jesus prayed for us, that we would glorify the Father because of our relationships with one another. He prayed for our ability to live in common with one another:

> May they all be one, as You, Father, are in Me and I am in
> You. May they also be one in Us, so the world may believe

You sent Me. I have given them the glory You have given Me. May they be one as We are one. I am in them and You are in Me. May they be made completely one, so the world may know You have sent Me and have loved them as You have loved Me. (John 17:21–23)

Community is a laboratory to study God's Word and to practice following His relationship principles in order to bring glory to Him. In open-ended interviews with people in groups, one of the consistent benefits we discovered was how group diversity helped people learn how to relate better. Here is a sample of their comments:

- Loving the outcast is hard but rewarding. Now I view everyone equally as God's child.
- The reason small groups turn into real friendships is because the common factor is Jesus, and He is never going to change.
- God has surely thrown out my preconceived notions about people and shown me that I have more in common with my small-group peers than I thought I would at first.

In summary, the Transformational Groups Manifesto is: (1) The Bible, (2) Gospel, (3) Mission, and (4) Grace.

The Right Culture for Community

So many churches are trying to get larger. They put a lot of time, energy, and money into their pursuit of getting bigger. The church needs to make getting small a priority. Church-health proponents are reminding pastors that the bigger the church gets, the smaller it has to get. In our research survey two-thirds of pastors told us they believe discipleship happens most effectively either one-on-one or in a group of fewer than five. Those pastors are on to something!

We want people gathered in worship, then in smaller groups. But we also want to push down further and have them in one-on-one discipling relationships. When we write about groups, we are using that term generically. They could be cell groups, home groups, Bible study classes, adult Bible fellowships, Sunday school classes, or accountability groups. We're less concerned about the place than we are about what they're doing, the purpose, and how they are accomplishing that purpose.

When it comes to group development, churches appear to be either prone to strategy or prone to organic experience. With strategy, churches can fall prey to an assembly-line mentality. With organic experience, they may never do anything. There is room for a third category: a strategic culture of community.

Sometimes *organic* is used to describe anything that happens unintentionally. It is erroneous to believe that anything ever happens just because it happens. Organic experiences are actually birthed out of the culture and the ethos that is developed in the church. Since most people who come to church are still enmeshed in the individualist mind-set, groups are not on their radar. Most pastors overestimate the willingness or desire of people to jump into small community.

We need to create systems that move people from being passive spectators to becoming active participants in small-group life. Having a system that says, "We track this," is important. Several computer programs are designed to help churches keep track of where people are in the process. They track first-time guests, second-time guests, whether they've been contacted, etc. But the idea is moving them toward a group.

Creating this culture involves more than the pastor saying, "OK, everybody move from rows to circles." They're not going to move because the pastor preaches a series about community or hangs a diagram on the wall. Belief followed by strategy and culture moves people to community.

We surveyed people who had left group life for whatever reason. We found a large number reported they would be willing to come back to a group, but they wanted more than just a weekly study. This indicates that their last group didn't deliver what they were expecting. They expected more than a study, but what they got was a study.

This is why over the last twenty years some of the group gurus emphasized the importance of relationships and shepherds. People who are doing life together aren't just going to group once a week; they are connecting throughout the week. They go out to movies and have dinner together. The group meeting is just one of the things they do. They also do life together and wrestle with tough questions. The group meeting is simply the time they gather. They are in community all week long. Community is not just Monday or Tuesday night for two hours; it is every day.

At Grace Church, the church where Ed pastors, the groups emphasize the *1-4-1* rhythm of community each month:

1 Social Activity
4 Group Meetings
1 Service Activity

That's the type of group we long to see in churches. If people are not experiencing this type of connection, they're fooling themselves with a false sense of community. If they are just going to church, watching the show, sitting there in rows, and facing forward like mindless automatons, they are missing community. The end result is that they are not experiencing the spiritual growth God has for them. The research is telling us that people want relationships and they're not getting them.

From the Group

There is a feeling of family in our small group. You don't feel like others are looking down on you when you comment or ask a question. For this year my goal was to do Bible study daily. So far I have done this. Through Bible study and small group, I feel that God is speaking to me, and I am listening even more.

—Dennis

What's Next?

- Consider writing your own Transformational Groups Manifesto or, if you like, borrow ours.
- Who can help you?
- How do you plan to use it to influence the values and culture of your groups?

2
Trees Don't Move the Wind

LeaderSpeak

> *Community is an instrument of worship, a weapon against sin, and a tool for evangelism—all for the exaltation of Jesus.*
> —Brad House, *Community*[1]

Next Step: *Assess the transformation platforms in your church.*

Brian[2] was influenced by a small group before he ever attended one. He was VP of sales development for a chemical company. His wife, Stacie, was attending a women's small group. Brian was amazed at how God was changing her life. Yet he had perfectly good reasons to avoid getting involved.

"My major fear about attending a small group was opening up with other guys and letting them see how weak I was spiritually," Brian said. But his desire to grow finally helped him take a big step and try a small group. Watching God at work in Stacie's life made him hungry for the same in his own life. "I saw how she was growing spiritually. . . . I just craved some of that as well."

When Brian tried a men's small group that met weekly at a coffee shop, he experienced something different from what he expected. He found men in the group who were just like him. "I discovered there were other guys just like me, which was very calming. We were all trying to grow spiritually," Brian said.

God is doing new things in Brian's life as a result of his involvement. "Now I am opening up more, praying more, reading my Bible more, and really taking the sermon to a different level," he explained. "In our small group we dig into the sermon a little further than you can in just an hour," he added. He described an "unexplainable void" in his life that God is now filling through his small-group connection.

Brian believes that anyone who tries a small group will make some of the same discoveries he has made. "I met real people, living real lives, with real problems, all there for the same purpose—to grow closer to God." Brian has led group meetings occasionally and serves on a weekly basis in his local church. For him small groups became God's platform for transformation. And that is what this book is all about.

Transformation Platforms

Churches have a problem. Our scorecard is not quite what it needs to be. We have long measured things in the church, but if our goal is to make disciples, we are not convinced that we have really measured what matters. We need a new scorecard for making disciples.

To that end, LifeWay Research surveyed 2,930 American adults who attend a Protestant church at least once a month in an effort to better understand effective disciple making and help the church create a new scorecard for measuring effectiveness. Within that research, however, we learned a tremendous amount about the importance of groups to the success of a church when it comes to making disciples. The research is compelling; God is using groups to bring about transformation in the lives of His people. If you can force yourself to look at stats for a moment, you will be struck with how significant biblical community is to the life of a believer.

The outcome of this research revealed eight areas of discipleship at work in maturing believers. Brian's story is strikingly similar to other stories from across the country who tell of how God has transformed everyday people using the platform of groups. Allow us, in the chapters ahead, to unpack these eight attributes, and show some statistical data that illustrates just how significant this transformative influence can be.

The eight areas of discipleship were:

1. Bible Engagement
2. Obeying God and Denying Self
3. Serving God and Others
4. Sharing Christ
5. Exercising Faith
6. Seeking God
7. Building Relationships
8. Unashamed (Transparency)

The research also provided insights on the differences among individuals who regularly attend groups. When we say "group," we are referring to a regular small gathering of believers that meet together to encourage one another toward growth and godliness. The "group" may be a home Bible study, a Sunday school class, or have a plethora of other names. Respondents were asked how often they attend small groups, Bible study classes, Sunday school groups, or adult Bible fellowships, etc. Using the results from this question, we noted a few specific subsets based off their frequency of attending a group.

For example, people who regularly attend groups show an increased level of commitment to building their individual relationships with Christ and with others. Attending a group is part of the "Building Relationships" attribute, meaning the more often one attends, the higher an individual scores in this area.

But the impact is seen across all other attributes. Those respondents who attend a group at least four times a month[3] show a significantly higher score in every area of discipleship compared with those who do not attend. In fact, the overall discipleship score for those who attend groups four times a month or more is 20 percent higher than those who do not attend groups. This is a significant difference and indicates the importance of groups to the task of making disciples.

While this shows the big-picture impact of groups, what is happening on a more individual level? Specific questions from the survey exhibit large differences in giving a "positive response."[4] For the "agree-disagree" scale the respondent typically must strongly or somewhat agree with the statement. In addition, some questions are worded from a negative perspective, and in those cases the respondent must strongly or somewhat disagree.

Brian is an example of this type of "positive response," at least based on his self-reported behavior. Review his story again and place numbers beside the attributes he reports from the eight areas of discipleship. Brian was unaware of the research. But he did report significant changes in his own life that included, but were not limited to, areas such as Bible engagement, seeking God, building relationships, and unashamed (transparency). He also demonstrated behaviors such as serving God and others, along with obeying God and denying self. Brian is convinced that the changes he experienced were directly related to his being in a group.

The table below shows the questions with the largest differences between those who attend groups at least four times a month and those who do not attend groups. All of these questions have at least a 25 percent difference between regular attenders and nonattenders, and that's a big deal for those of us wanting a healthy church.

Take a look at these charts and let the numbers sink in.

Question	Did not attend a group	Attended a group 4+ times a month
I intentionally spend time with other believers in order to help them grow in their faith.	22%	63%
I have developed significant relationships with people at my church.	57%	89%
I am intentionally putting my spiritual gift(s) to use serving God and others.	42%	73%
I intentionally try to get to know new people I meet at church.	37%	67%
Throughout the day I find myself thinking about biblical truths.	45%	74%
Spiritual matters do not tend to come up as a normal part of my daily conversations with other Christians.	38%	19%
If a person is sincerely seeking God, he/she can obtain eternal life through religions other than Christianity.	33%	18%

Group involvement makes attendees more likely to be intentional in spending time with other believers. There is greater than a 40 percent difference between the two groups when measuring the effort to intentionally make time for fellowship with other believers and to intentionally spend time with other believers to help spiritual growth. This should not be surprising, since these individuals are already making an effort by attending groups. In the group survey that will be discussed in detail later, the most common reasons people stopped attending or do not currently attend groups stem from time constraints. This choice impacts other parts of their spiritual walk. Regular attendees are also more intentional about putting their spiritual gifts to use, and in addition, they are getting to know new people at their churches.

Group involvement impacts people's daily lives. Group attenders are more likely to find themselves thinking about biblical truths throughout the day. Additionally, spiritual matters are a normal part of their daily conversations with other Christians. These examples show how those involved in groups tend to spend more time thinking and discussing biblical and spiritual matters. Finally, group attenders are negatively impacted when they have not read the Bible. There is a 33 percent difference in feeling unfulfilled if survey respondents go several days without reading the Bible.

For the following table, respondents were asked about how often they did the listed activities (not including times these activities are done as part of a church worship service). The table shows the percentage who selected either every day or a few times a week for the frequency of performing each activity.

Again, the differences are striking. Our research confirms our belief that small groups are needed for greater effectiveness in discipleship.

Those respondents who attend groups are spending significantly more time reading and studying the Bible. This is not simply a reflection of reading and studying the Bible during a group meeting. Responses were at a higher frequency than the respondents' weekly attendance. The results were for reading and studying at least a few times a week compared with attending a group about once a week.

Additionally, those individuals regularly attending groups are more actively praying. Whether it is for the church and its leaders, with other Christians, for fellow Christians, or for those who are not professing Christians, regular attendees are praying at least a few times a week at a much higher percentage than those who do not attend a group.

Spiritual Discipline	Did not attend a group	Attended a group 4+ times a month
Read the Bible	27%	67%
Pray for my church and/or church leaders	30%	64%
Study the Bible	10%	42%
Pray in a group with other Christians	7%	36%
Pray for fellow Christians I know	54%	82%
Pray for the spiritual status of people I know who are not professing Christians	35%	60%
Confess my sins and wrongdoings to God and ask for forgiveness	54%	79%

Finally, regular attendees are more diligent in confessing sins and wrongdoings. You may say, "Maybe regular attendees sin more." Hopefully this isn't the case, but if it is, we are glad they are in a group that will help them grow past their sinful habits! We are suggesting that, in either case, as Christians grow, they become more aware of their wrongdoings and less satisfied with the sins in their lives.

Another set of questions within the discipleship survey asked respondents to give the number of times they had taken specific actions within the last six months. Once again, the table below shows where there are significant differences between respondents who regularly attend small groups and those who do not attend.

Simply put, it makes sense that people in groups have higher community relationships in the church. But, as we have seen, they also have greater discipleship practices outside small groups. But now we see that it impacts the fact that we reach out to others, give, pray, and so much more—being in small-group community leads to living on mission. Notice the difference between those who attended a small group (SG). The differences on the number of times they had taken action in a specific behavioral characteristic action in the last six months are dramatic.

This doesn't imply that attending groups is the sole key attribute in discipleship. In other areas of discipleship there is little to no difference between those who attend a group regularly and those who do not. But the overwhelming evidence supports the idea that a difference occurs for those who regularly attend groups.

While we cannot say that attending the group is the reason for the differences, one thing is definitely clear:

> *Those who attend groups act and*
> *think differently from those who do not.*

We passionately believe that engaging in small groups is not just connected (as the data proves), but our experience is that it also promotes and even causes such greater involvement and activity. That's been our experience, and it is why we wrote this book.

Our passion is not propped up by statistics alone. As church practitioners, we have seen stories like Brian's over and over. These stories are not limited to married white-collar businessmen who are VPs of their companies. People from every demographic and cultural background worldwide have experienced the transformative power of God through the small-groups platform. We believe a return or advancement to a committed embracing of small groups can be transformational for your church and community—for God's glory and for His mission.

Behavior that is characteristic of a growing disciple.	Did not attend a group	Attended a group 4+ times a month
Shared with someone how to become a Christian	0.68	2.30
Invited an unchurched person to attend a church service or some other program at your church	0.88	3.18
Attended a worship service at your church	3.24	5.60
Made a decision to obey or follow God with an awareness that choosing His way might be costly to you in some way	2.40	5.12
Fasted	0.33	1.11
Memorized a Bible verse	1.08	3.23

Behavior that is characteristic of a growing disciple.	Did not attend a group	Attended a group 4+ times a month
About what percentage of your total annual income (before taxes) do you contribute to your local church?	6.07%	10.34%
Are you currently involved in ministries or projects that serve people in the community that are not affiliated with your church?	26%	47%
Do you currently have regular responsibilities at your church (for example: greeter, teacher, musician, etc.)?	25%	63%

Do your regular responsibilities in your church include teaching or mentoring other people (i.e., are you a Sunday school teacher, Bible study leader, youth group teacher, etc.)?	22%	56%

Building the Right Tree

Before we continue to make our case and deliver information we believe can help you, some clarity is critical. I (Ed) have a few "Ed-isms" I tend to say repeatedly. They're usually short, pithy, and representative of a core value I believe regarding the local church or the Christian faith. For example:

The trees don't move the wind.

We're referring to the heresy created when churches (and their leaders) try to simply follow a formula in order to produce the "perfect church." They want the Holy Spirit to move in a mighty way that creates astounding church growth, life, and health . . . just as He did somewhere else.

We want the Holy Spirit to move, too, but we are mistaken if we believe that if we build our "tree" just right, we will be able to control a movement of God's Spirit. Consider the example of Evan Roberts, who witnessed one of the greatest revivals in history. The famous Welsh Revival in 1904 resulted in an estimated 100,000 people coming to Christ in six months. There is more to the story, but any of us would be pleased to start with those kinds of results in our cities and communities.

We all can relate to Roberts' famous prayer: "Lord, bend me." But we can relate even more to the second part of his prayer, which says, "Lord, bend the church, save the world." We live in a world that is desperate for saving, but God's transformational platform is a church that must be bent in order to be leveraged to save. We are optimistic about the potential and power of the local church. Yet, apart from the wind of God, there are no trees of any value that we can build.

We must resist becoming like the prophets of Baal on Mount Carmel, building our own altars and dancing around them frantically as we beg our "god" to send fire (see 1 Kings 18:20–40). No structures, institutions, programs, or processes—including groups—can inherently "move the wind" or manufacture fire from heaven.

The prophet Zechariah is another example of the principle that trees don't move the wind. This prophet's word from God to a beleaguered King Zerubbabel was a reminder. God's Spirit—which was the Hebrew word *ruach* for "breath" or "wind"—was the key to the king's success at building something great. And it was not simply the God of the universe quietly exhaling, although that would seem to be plenty. God forcefully pushed the wind of His Spirit into the situation:

> "Not by strength or by might, but by My Spirit," says the
> LORD of Hosts. "What are you, great mountain? Before
> Zerubbabel you will become a plain." (Zech. 4:6–7)

God spoke to the prophet in everyday terms: "Your human strength and military force won't be the secrets to your success—God's power will be." The same will be true for all of us. The trees don't move the wind.

We are not inviting you on a mystical journey from here on out, although you might be wondering at this point. What we are saying is that leaders cannot enforce, impose, or implement God's will. However, we do think it's important for church leaders to prayerfully assess and restructure, if necessary, the way their churches look or function in order to make more and better disciples.

Since Jesus calls us to make disciples (Matt. 28:18–20) we must pray, think, and then plan about how to do that most effectively.

Catch the Spirit's Wind

Having said this, it's important to note that our systems should not be in opposition to God's Word or God's movement. While the trees don't move the wind, God did intentionally design trees in such a way that their branches and leaves could catch the wind when it blows. God can help us design systems with the purpose of giving Him space to make transformed disciples. Disciple making is the Spirit's work, but our work is to develop an intentional plan to allow the Spirit's work to be most effective. An old proverb says, "You can't control the wind, but you can adjust your sails." The Spirit may be blowing, but you may need to adjust the sails on your groups system to catch the Spirit's wind.

Revelation 2–3 clearly gives us biblical examples of assessing results and making midcourse corrections in local churches. Jesus comes to a church, presents His credentials, lists the church's strengths, examines the weaknesses, and designates a path to renewal. When we look more closely at His observations, we discover that Jesus, the church interventionist, commends hard work and persistence, but those characteristics are not enough to get a complete bill of health. You can do the right thing the wrong way. Further action was needed.

One example in this passage was the hardworking church of Ephesus. When you read Jesus' numerous compliments to this church, you might wonder why it was getting this 360° examination at all. They hated evil and refused to quit in the face of opposition. They were standing under intense pressure from the pagan culture of Ephesus. But something was missing that was vital to every other thing:

> But I have this against you: You have abandoned the love you had at first. Remember then how far you have fallen; repent, and do the works you did at first. Otherwise, I will come to you and remove your lampstand from its place— unless you repent. (Rev. 2:4–5)

Jesus had something "against" a church that seemed to be doing so many things well. Eight attributes were mentioned and commended. In spite of the fact that they were doing the right things, their motivation was in question.

You can do all the right things the wrong way.

The Ephesian church had literally fallen out of love with people and with Jesus. The purpose of the letter was to reveal blind spots—so this assessment was vital to their future. What was compelling them to keep moving forward? We are left to speculate about reasons ranging from religious discipline to the desire to win or be successful. But they had the wrong scorecard, and Jesus made that clear to them.

However, none of the seven churches, including Ephesus, deserved to be "thrown under the bus." Six of them were complimented. All of them were important enough to be spoken to by Jesus. And all were significant enough to be challenged to act and commanded to listen.

We are not pathological contrarians when it comes to the local church. The local church is God's platform to launch missionaries and rescue humanity for His own glory. God loves the local church!

Because we love the church and have invested most of our lives in her mission, we imagine better days. We do what we do because we believe the local church in America is worth talking to and is by no means a hopeless cause. And remember, to disparage the church and dismiss her relevance is to do the same to the God of the church and the head of the church—Jesus Christ. To paraphrase the church fathers, the church is a mess, but she is Christ's bride.

For some reason, however, whenever we discuss the practice of assessing and studying the church, it often generates some controversy. People argue, "Why do we even need a scorecard for churches? Why can't we just be faithful?"

Negativity toward evaluating a church is common, as is pessimism toward research in general when it comes to the things of

God. What scares us so much about taking a closer look at the results from our local churches? The mission of God is our sacred task, and the local church is the delivery system for missionaries within the mission.

I (Ed) grew up outside New York City when it was falling apart. One of the keys to turning it around was in mayors asking hard questions. Mayor Ed Koch was the famous and popular mayor of New York City from 1978 to 1989. One thing he was known for was walking through the offices of New York City Hall and asking random employees, "How am I doing?" He could ask this of a janitor, a secretary, or a manager. Now that took courage. No wonder he was so popular.

If we really care about the effectiveness of the church wherever God has assigned us, we will continually ask the tough questions. And we will not limit posing those tough questions to our best friends or special consultants. Neither will we ask them only a week or two out of the year. We will ask the janitor at our church or the convenience store clerk closest to our church. And we will ask them often. Why? Because we care about transformed people, and we care courageously.

As president of LifeWay Research (Ed), it's not surprising that I would see the value of research. I think it's completely appropriate to use a spiritually discerning process that is undergirded by an understanding of the marks of a biblical church. I have written books that have used such a process to analyze and evaluate more than seven thousand churches around the country and the world. The end result is that we get a bigger picture of what God is doing and how He is working through the church.

Certain wings of the theological world would contend that these sorts of evaluations just don't matter. I think to make such a statement is an overreaction to the Church Growth Movement, specifically when people became consumed with "methodological mania." While research-based books and studies by no means guarantee or should make us think the trees move the wind, they can give us constructive insights and principles.

Groups and Transformation

Groups have been part of local churches for some time, though in a myriad of forms. You may call it small groups or Sunday school or missional communities, but most churches have a form of groups. We are convinced that groups are vital, but we refuse to declare any one form of groups to be the "killer app" or ultimate solution for your local church.

Apple claims it has with their app store slogan: *Hundreds of Thousands of Endless Possibilities.* Apple is describing more than 775,000 mini-applications or "apps" for its iPads, iPhones, and iPods. The online store is replete with apps that address pain points, meet needs, and entertain us. Apple can fix your life, or so it thinks.

Churches seem to have almost as many apparent solutions that will inspire people to attend. Leaders torture themselves in search of the next "solution" or formula or group format that will cause people to flock to them by the masses. Yet formulas that magically increase church attendance are rare in the world, particularly if part of your scorecard is to reach the previously unchurched. And even if a magical formula would increase church attendance and ultimately attendance in group meetings, not all approaches make mature disciples.

If we are not careful, by saying that groups are "the solution" for a church that wants to grow and effectively reach a community, we can become guilty of creating another tree. And we all know that trees don't move the wind, right? We are only feeding our fascination with formulas and secrets to success.

Years ago some church experts declared parking, programs, and space as the secrets to numerical success. And although at the time we said it was for all the right reasons (evangelism, etc.), this was lost when our formulas seemed to produce impressive results.

We all became Little League baseball players again, crowded around our buddy who just hit a home run, clamoring to use his bat. Someone's formula paid off, and no matter our context, gifts, or abilities, we were going to step up to the plate with a new bat in our hands—one that some "all-star" pastor used with favorable results.

The church planter in an elementary school near you may have the vision to birth the next great arena-sized church. So the planter desperately searches for the formulas of the big and famous. How do they preach? How do they worship? How do they structure ministries for preschoolers, children, youth, and first-time attenders? Rarely does this copy-paste syndrome produce the same results in other contexts.

During the search for success and significance, it becomes apparent to this church planter that one specific form of groups is a "big deal." This application solves every problem a thriving local church could face. From communication to becoming known and from attendee retention to pastoral care, this one form of group is a dream come true to the large-church dreamer. Mimicking language, teaching styles, and processes only brings frustration to everyone involved.

A church planter met with a coach to help figure out how to establish leaders who would oversee the church's community group structure. When asked how many people were participating in groups, the planter said about half. That was a good start. To get an idea of the scope, the planter was asked how many attended the church. The response was approximately twenty-five to thirty people. The church WAS a small group. They did not need the structure that the planter read about from a popular megachurch. The planter was mimicking someone else's church rather than ministering to their own church.

Throughout this book you will read references to the plethora of benefits a robust group ministry provides for a healthy local church. But vibrant groups are not simply an idea of the local church. Smaller groups are a well-documented sociological phenomenon outside the church as well. Seth Godin refers to these as "Tribes."

You can have a visually striking group ministry complete with impressive leaders and a long line of people clamoring to attend. But for what purpose? To grow your church and save your staff from compassion fatigue? Or is it for a higher goal?

The ultimate target of a group is spiritual, not sociological. Our human inclination to avoid aloneness will cause some of us to find value in smaller groups of people, no matter their purpose. And churches can be driven for all kinds of reasons to have a vigorous and specific group bent. Leaders have to consistently remind people why they are expected to be involved in community.

Laying groundwork for a group scorecard is vital. Our measurement is not the number of groups or the number of people in groups. It is not the form of the groups, nor is our scorecard tallied through the number of satisfied group customers.

Our target for groups is:

More and deeper disciples making more and deeper disciples for God's glory and His mission.

Living in community with other believers, wrestling through real issues, embracing the gospel together, reminding one another of our identity in Christ, lovingly holding one another accountable for involvement in the spiritual disciplines, and watching the way authentic Christians do life is God's transformative platform. Jesus lived in community with the apostles. He didn't gloat about the large crowds that came to hear Him preach. Rather, He emphasized the development of twelve men over the course of three years. He sought to transform their beliefs, their faith, and their practices. After His resurrection He commissioned them to take up this ministry of transformation with all types of people.

People secretly crave transformation. The self-help section of your local Books-A-Million is crammed full of books containing steps and formulas for a better life. This is not an ungodly pursuit, provided our desire is for the right type of transformation—the kind where God receives the glory. The before and after picture of people transformed by God allows Him to receive glory inside and outside the church walls.

Transformation for a Purpose

Transformation is central to the mission of God. John 20:21 reminds us—as Jesus was sent by God, so He sends us! But the mission of God is not simply being sent somewhere—the mission of God is being sent somewhere *to do something*: "If you forgive the sins of any, they are forgiven them; if you retain the sins of any, they are retained" (John 20:23).

Missionaries were given the authority through the Holy Spirit to declare the forgiveness of Christ. Again the mission is not just being sent. If our wives send us to the grocery store to pick up chips and drinks for our small-group meeting, we best not leave and come home empty-handed. We can use the wimpy excuse, "But you told us to go, and we did; what is the problem?" We were not sent for the sake of being sent; we were sent so that something specific would take place (buying chips and drinks for small group).

We want to say this with clarity: groups are about living in the gospel, not simply about living together or serving the community. If missional activity is all about good intentions and just doing something, then the gospel mission is betrayed. Transformational groups include all three essential elements: gospel, community, and mission.

When groups serve the community without going in the name of and speaking the name of Jesus, they are simply carrying out works of justice. There is no such thing as covert Christianity.

The powerful message of transformation begins with the forgiveness of sins. And what is even more compelling about the passage above is that our refusal to be sent is the same as our denying forgiveness and transformation.

Jesus' mission is transformation. The late D. James Kennedy, described as the "most listened to Presbyterian minister in the world," discussed the transforming influence of Christ upon society:

When Jesus took upon Himself the form of man, He imbued mankind with a dignity and inherent value that had never been dreamed of before. Whatever Jesus touched or whatever He did transformed that aspect of human life. Many people will read about the innumerable small incidents in the life of Christ while never dreaming that those casually mentioned "little" things were to transform the history of mankind.[5]

So we want groups that lead to transformation—transformational groups.

Spiritual transformation in the lives of people will result in greater compassion for the challenges other people face in everyday life. Transformational people have a new sensitivity to societal injustice and a greater motivation to see substantive change. When we say "transformation" or "transformational," we are not talking about a nebulous, synergistic, or mystical phenomenon. We are talking about what happens when God's power changes (and continues to change) individuals—and through those individuals changes the surrounding environment.

This familiar passage gives a picture of transformation as an ongoing process: "Do not be conformed to this age, but be *transformed* by the renewing of your mind, so that you may discern what is the good, pleasing, and perfect will of God" (Rom. 12:2). Christ followers experience a supernatural shaping, or formation, process.

But this process is a specific type of change. Paul's information helps us see that all shaping is not from God. We are always being shaped by something, either by the world's way of thinking or by God's power. The person or object I am closest to shapes me. (If you see some guy's head start to look like a football or a golf ball, you'll know what happened!)

Paul describes an ongoing process that includes being fully available to God. The spiritual transformation process involves deep and continual change. Even as a Christian we will be close to someone or something. When we are close to God, we will be re-formed, or transformed, into His shape.

In Christ we have an opportunity for deep, qualitative re-formation. "Now the Lord is the Spirit, and where the Spirit of the Lord is, there is freedom. We all, with unveiled faces, are looking as in a mirror at the glory of the Lord and are being *transformed* into the same image from glory to glory; this is from the Lord who is the Spirit" (2 Cor. 3:17–18).

The root of the word *transformed* is used in another place in Scripture. Paul said to the Galatian Christians, "My children, I am again suffering labor pains for you until Christ is *formed* in you" (Gal. 4:19). Paul used the metaphor of fetal development to describe spiritual transformation. The embryo begins as an unrecognizable form of life inside a female and becomes a fully formed human being.

Now we not only get a valuable picture of God's process of discipleship, but we also find a scriptural foundation for what God really wants. God wants to change the form of those who follow Him into the form of His Son, Jesus. We don't start off looking like a fully formed, Christlike person. The formation takes place over time.

Much more than an unchurched person becoming churched or an irreligious person finding religion, this happens when Christ re-forms someone beyond recognition. We are talking about death and rebirth into an entirely new life form (2 Cor. 5:17). Christ lives in believers who decide to follow Him. Then these believers take up residence in their communities and the world. Transformation is God's work deep within the believer that makes him or her genuinely like Jesus.

Transformation is not, fundamentally, our work. It is God's. Why? Well, because the gospel is not "you do"; it's "Jesus did." He did His work, redeeming and saving, and then He created a people for Himself—a people to be on mission—together. Another term often used for *discipleship* or *spiritual growth* is "spiritual formation." Originally, the term *morphoo* or "formed" was used to describe artists who shaped their materials into various images. God does the work of shaping us. It is our responsibility to allow our lives to be formed by the Master. Isaiah declares, "Yet Lord, You are our Father; we are the clay, and You are our potter; we all are the work of Your hands" (Isa. 64:8). We do this best in community together by applying all the "one anothers" of Scripture.

Old Testament Groups

Go back to the beginning of Genesis to get a picture of the first instance of human community as God brought Adam and Eve together because He determined that it was not good for man to be alone. However, just because you have a people gathered together, doesn't mean you experience "togetherness" or *commūnitās* (Latin meaning "in common"). The garden was an example of perfect community. All relationships and rules were mutual, as were goals.

Former atheist turned Christian apologist, Alister McGrath, sees man's innate desire for community as a "clue" to the existence of God. "Relationality" leverages Christianity beyond a religious or ideological debate. In reference to the biblical story of Adam and Eve, McGrath said:

> We see here a recognition of the relationality of human beings. We have been created to exist in relationship—with one another, and with God. . . . To be authentically human is to exist in relationship—as we are meant to.[6]

A theology of community begins here because we were created for community. So when we recreate biblical community, we are returning people to the environment for which God created us. Community is a sociological phenomenon as well for the same reason—people, no matter their tongue, tribe, or nation, were not created to do life alone: "Then the LORD God said, 'It is not good for the man to be alone. I will make a helper as his complement'" (Gen. 2:18).

That's big—foundational—to all human existence. And it was not just about a husband and wife (as that verse is often referenced). It did not say, "It is not good for a man to be single." God said, "It is not good for the man to be *alone*." We need others.

People will find community somewhere, whether it is at the local bar, golf course, or book club. People will Facebook their way through life if that is their only option. Adam and Eve found community with each other because, for Adam, to be alone was "not good" in God's eyes.

Adam and Eve could be described with all the group clichés we use today. They "did life together" in a great group environment. Although they had responsibilities, the group seemed to be organic versus highly structured.

Adam evidently communicated truth to Eve. The one rule of the group came from God to Adam: "But you must not eat from the tree of the knowledge of good and evil, for on the day you eat from it, you will certainly die" (Gen. 2:17). And in some way God communicated this to Eve also—either through Adam to Eve or to her directly.

But something got lost in translation. Either Eve misremembered or Adam miscommunicated. What happened at the exact moment of Eve's moral collapse is unclear. Was Adam watching the whole time and failed to interrupt her conversation with Satan? Or was Adam somewhere else, seemingly neglecting his responsibility? We don't get the small details but just the big picture.

Some of the details we don't have in Bible stories are tantalizing. But one point is clear. The failure of Adam and Eve—their sin with incredible consequences—was the result of a failure to live in community with God and each other. The Bible makes clear the community, God's presence, and the brokenness that came to all of it.

Adam and Eve's failure to live in community was seen in their first response to sin: a colossal cover-up . . . hiding themselves from each other (fig leaves) and hiding themselves from God "among the trees of the garden" (Gen. 3:8). By hiding, they lost what they needed most: love, restoration, and grace. They wanted to become invisible when what they really needed was to be found! We respond in similar ways.

Our sin nature drives us to hide from community. People love to live in secret. Yet community becomes the place where light can shine on the dark places of our lives. Religion is the great cover-up, but community is the place where "you will know the truth, and the truth will set you free" (John 8:32). As we have said before, secrets and grace cannot coexist, so abundant life with Christ always involves removing a lid. The lid is made of our secrets.

Fear keeps people out of community with God and others. And fear is the primary reason people avoid connecting with groups in your church. People fear not fitting in, being put on the spot, or being judged. A robust group connection process will address some of the fears that keep people away from group life. But the greatest advertisement for small-group participation is transformation. People need to see that it really makes a significant difference in their lives to walk in the light with others.

The first question from God recorded in the Bible was addressed to Adam and Eve: "Where are you?" (Gen. 3:9). Did God have trouble finding Adam and Eve? Were they that good at hiding? Obviously God knew more about Adam and Eve than they knew about themselves. And God called them out of their own blindness. He can use groups to do the same thing. Community is not the only way for people to be invited out of hiding, but in the right group the possibilities for this become much greater.

When God found Adam and Eve, the grace and restoration process began. Don't miss the point here—the consequences of their choice are well documented. But life with God went on afterwards, and their community grew—both in number and in complexity. Mankind has been in this struggle between secrecy and community with God and others ever since.

Community is hard . . . and essential.

New Testament Groups

About three thousand people were saved at Pentecost, but they didn't all go to the same church after this event; in fact, many of them did not stay in the same city for very long. They were in Christian communities that met in homes. And although they gathered in the synagogue daily, it's highly unlikely that they were ever in a gathering that large again.

The churches of the New Testament weren't really our size. The median attendance of a church in the U.S. is seventy-five people; that statistic includes more than sixteen hundred megachurches of two thousand attenders or more. The first church building did not exist for many decades after the resurrection and the formation of the church.

In addition, for a long time before that, Christians were seen as a sect (like a break-off denomination) of the Jews. So they would gather in the temple with other Jewish believers. The Bible says they met in the temple and from house to house. The temple isn't the same thing as a church today, but the idea has some connection.

When they did not meet in the temple (there was only one and it was in Jerusalem), they met in the synagogue and, in all likelihood, in homes. Christians would later be expelled from the synagogues, and they eventually met in larger and larger groups (eventually building their own buildings). However, the best expressions always had times and places where they met in small communities for mutual encouragement and accountability.

So there were both large- and small-group functions in the New Testament church and the churches that followed. History supports the idea that most of the churches in the New Testament functioned as house churches. Clement of Rome, who many believe is the Clement mentioned by Paul in Philippians 4:3, became the first bishop of Rome. He wrote his sermons and sent them out to all the small house churches around Rome.

Daily life for new Holy Spirit-filled Christ followers radically changed. The rhythm of life was built around a daily connection with God and fellow believers:

> Every day they devoted themselves to meeting together in the temple complex, and broke bread from house to house. They ate their food with a joyful and humble attitude, praising God and having favor with all the people. And every day the Lord added to them those who were being saved. (Acts 2:46–47)

These Christians were doing much more than meeting. Faith was integrated into their lives every day. Jesus was not following them; they were following Him. Everything changed.

The early church moved well beyond meeting out of religious obligation or in order to check a dutiful box. Something incredibly transformative was happening as they prayed, worshipped, broke bread, and saw God do amazing things every day.

You can't use Acts 2:42–47 as a proof text or a theological basis for groups, but neither do we want to ignore the description found there. The organic impulse of people who follow Jesus is to follow Him together. As the early Christians followed Him together, a new community environment was formed, which God used for the purpose of transformation:

> Now all the believers were *together* and held all things in *common.* (Acts 2:44)

Practically speaking, that could not possibly be done every day in a crowd of three thousand. Eventually faith trickled down to every room these winsome new believers entered—including their own homes. A supernatural sense of togetherness emerged, and people grew exponentially. Simply put, to follow Christ all alone is unchristian. If we are connected to Christ, we are connected intimately to other believers as well:

Now as we have many parts in one body, and all the parts
do not have the same function, in the same way we who are
many are one body in Christ and individually members of
one another. (Rom. 12:4–5)

This rhythm of life continued throughout the New Testament.
The large gathering/smaller group pattern was evident as Christians
lived out their faith together:

Every day in the temple complex, and in various homes,
they continued teaching and proclaiming the good news
that Jesus is the Messiah. (Acts 5:42)

We think that is a rhythm Christians should still follow today.
Are groups structured in such a way to facilitate this rhythm?

The State of Groups

We believe groups (or classes, Bible fellowships, etc.) should be
important to churches because God has supernaturally ordained
community to sanctify His people. In other words groups provide
environments for people to grow in Christ. God, who is an eternal
community of three persons, created community for our benefit and
His glory.

And smaller groups help believers live in community with one
another.

That is why we are making a big deal about groups and why
there is this new book in the Transformational Church series—
Transformational Groups. Groups are about God's desire to transform His followers for His glory. His desire is also our desire.

Though most pastors say groups are important, our research
revealed that for many churches there's a major discrepancy between
the stated importance of groups and the actual working reality of
that importance. For many churches, contrary to what is articulated,
groups are really not that important. We think this is a problem.

At least two alarming facts were discovered:

1. *Group content is treated haphazardly in many churches.* The majority of pastors and church leaders have no clue what is being studied. As stated earlier, almost two-thirds of pastors tell us that the person primarily responsible for selecting the curriculum for the group is the group leader. A large number of those do so without any oversight or direction from the pastor or staff. In most cases not only are group leaders not given studies built on a theology and discipleship strategy, but they are also not given anything at all—not a plan or a recommended resource list—nothing.

Now if the church has a group training mechanism in place on the front end, and if group leaders are vetted theologically, this might make sense. They should be taught to choose resources in accordance with the theology of the church. Hopefully they are also equipped to think strategically about spiritual growth plans for their groups. If so, then handing the responsibility to the group leader would be proper empowerment.

If, however, the above is not in existence, there is ministry negligence. A wise pastor would never treat the teaching from the pulpit with that type of haphazard planning. And group content should not be treated this way either. As a leader, you must see groups as integral to the plan of your church, focused on the direction God has given your church, and aligned with the beliefs of your church.

You simply must care about the content being studied in groups.

One way to be certain group leaders are using resources that are in line with a church's theology is to give each leader the websites of a few publishing companies whose theology is in line with the church you lead. Let the group leaders know that they can choose any resource from any of those publishing companies. Also tell the same group leaders that, if they would like to use something from a publisher other than the ones listed, the resource will need to be cleared by the group pastor or leadership team.

Some may say that the church has too much oversight or that they are being micromanagers by involving themselves this deeply in the choice of curriculum. This is just not so. The reason great pastors are involved in resource choices is so nothing heretical is taught and no false teachings are espoused. Believe me, cleaning up theological messes after the fact is much more difficult than catching them before they dirty up someone's biblical worldview.

2. *The majority of church attenders don't believe groups are that important to the church.* Though pastors say groups are important to the church, regrettably the majority of church attenders don't say the same thing. In other words, in many churches the importance of groups is largely an aspirational value for church leaders and not an actual value in the culture of the church. Church leaders should ask themselves why the people in the church do not consider groups to be more important. The following questions could be helpful to consider:

- Are the pastors and leaders in groups or leading a group?
- Do the people in the church continually hear about groups?
- If someone wanted to join a group today, what would you tell them to do?
- Are stories of transformation that occur in community shared with the church?
- In comparison to the weekend services, how much energy is poured into group strategy, leader training, etc.?
- Is there a clear path for the attenders of a weekend service to get from the pew to a group, from sitting in rows to sitting in circles?
- Are your groups available for anyone who wants to participate, or is there a waiting period?
- Does the church conduct an annual churchwide campaign to promote groups and get people into groups?
- Are other ministry leaders (staff members, women's ministry leaders, men's ministry leaders, etc.) encouraging those in their ministries to be involved in a group?
- Does the church's schedule allow busy people the time to do life together in community?

The reality is that most church leaders devote much more energy to the worship services than to groups. Caring less about the worship gathering is not the point; caring more about groups is. In worship gatherings grounded in Jesus, God supernaturally uses the preaching of His Word and the worship to transform hearts and affections. And in groups grounded in Jesus, God supernaturally uses the community to mature His people. Both are important to God. Both must be important to your church.

From the Group

God frees us when we are honest with ourselves and ask our friends to pray for a struggle we would prefer to keep secret. My best friends in life are people I met in my small group. We have shed tears together and celebrated life's reward together.

—David

What Now?

- What change can you make to refocus your church on groups?
- How can your groups be retooled for greater transformation?

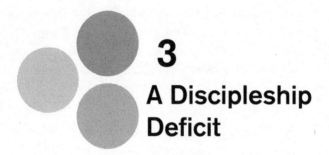

3
A Discipleship Deficit

LeaderSpeak

> *Clarifying what you want people to become will*
> *ultimately define your church's mission.*
> —Andy Stanley and Bill Willits, *Creating Community*[1]

> *Let him who is not in community beware of being alone.*
> *Into the community you were called, the call was not*
> *meant for you alone; in the community of the called you*
> *bear your cross, you struggle, you pray.*
> —Dietrich Bonhoeffer, *Life Together*

Next Step: *Design a community disciple-making strategy for your church.*

Galena Bible Church in Galena, Alaska, was literally a small group. Five and a half years ago a total of eight people were attending the church. The body did not have a pastor for three years, so it survived with DVDs, guest preachers, and members sharing what they were learning through personal devotions.

The challenge was compounded because Galena Bible Church is the only Protestant church for almost three hundred miles in any direction. Ugly infighting, inappropriate church discipline, and an almost complete lack of life involvement outside of church was part of GBC's history. But during those three years without a pastor, God began to teach the group what it meant to forgive one another, love one another, and engage in loving the community.

When Chris Kopp became their missionary-supported pastor, church attendance grew to the forties on Sundays. In the years following many have come to faith in Jesus, and the church has grown to the seventies and eighties in an isolated and inaccessible Alaskan native community of about five hundred.

Pastor Kopp explains that in the Athabaskan Indian language there is no word for *forgive*. Even though most of the population speaks only English, the cultural implications are still in play. Galena Bible Church had a native elder man named Val who was deeply hated by many in the community for terrible things he had done in his twenties. But this man had heard the gospel and responded in repentance and faith. In his mid-eighties Val's body gave out, and he went to be with the Lord. There is no funeral home in Galena, so every aspect of burial is left up to the community. Pastor Chris Kopp described what happened next:

> Because of his past, very few natives were willing to help in his burial, but the men of our church washed him, dressed him, built his casket, helped to dig the grave, did the funeral, and helped to bury him. The response from the community was one of amazement and gratitude. They had never seen a small group like this love someone who was not biologically related. They've been able to see that he was our brother, and we will see him again.

Transformation is what God wants. It is not limited to individuals, but entire communities can experience the power of God when they see powerful demonstrations of the gospel like in Galena. Jesus did not come to build a religion but to start a transformational movement. Neither did He come because He loved smaller groups and really wanted to start one. He came because of places like Galena and the people there—and places like your city and community.

His mission was simple—He came to serve, give, seek, and save:

- "For even the Son of Man did not come to be served, but to serve, and to give His life—a ransom for many" (Mark 10:45).
- "For the Son of Man has come to seek and to save the lost" (Luke 19:10).

Jesus' mission is now our mission. In His own words, "As the Father has sent Me, I also send you" (John 20:21). So, as simple and focused as was Jesus' mission, ours should be too. We exist to serve, to give, and to proclaim the saving work of Jesus Christ, regardless of the merit of those we serve.

You may love groups and have been deeply formed through your experience in them. Yet for groups to really work for God's glory and mission, they can never be the ultimate goal.

Transformation is the goal. Groups are the tool.

When people at Galena Bible Church were in community, they saw transformation. When they saw transformation, it was because they were on mission. They are all connected. Their mission was not to start a small group but to display the works of Jesus in community to others—even those who were despised. Transformation was the goal, and their group of believers became the tool to win the well-calloused hearts of the natives.

Start with Why

In his book *Start with Why,* business guru Simon Sinek reminds us of a simple concept that has been around a long time. We simply are not clear about "why" we do what we do. He communicates with great clarity how this often causes problems in business and in church. We get so infatuated with the "what" and the "how" that we miss the most important point—the "why" or the belief and purpose that drives what we do.[2]

Small groups (or insert the name of a similar environment at your church) have existed for some time. For many they represent a positive spiritual history. So because the assumption is that everyone will benefit from a smaller group experience, the challenge is to get them there. In most churches there is a group of experienced champions for groups. But unless groups are directly connected with the overall mission of God, their effectiveness in transformation will be limited.

Neal McGlohon, a leadership coaching specialist, explains his "why" and how it relates to groups:

> If God's heart and our vision is for every man, woman, and child in a community then why isn't that the stated reason for everything we do? Why do we reinforce people's natural tendency to "join" a group for relationships so they won't be lonely or uncared for? Although disciples caring for disciples are important, the only chance for movement is to mobilize transformed people into lost culture.[3]

Groups exist and flourish for all kinds of reasons. Great by-products of group life, such as caring for one another, can enhance God's mission. But the big question for leaders is:

Why do you want groups to exist in your world?

Signing up church members and making disciples is not the same thing. A lingering by-product of the Church Growth Movement is the idea that numeric growth is the ultimate goal of any church. Because of this, many church leaders ask themselves this question: what does it take to get someone to stick? That is, to get a guest attending a weekend worship service to visit our church, then become a member of our church.

One of the facts that has come to the forefront is that people will stick if their close friends are at the same church. And where is the best setting in which to make close friends? The answer is in a group. Because of this fact many church leaders, if they were being honest with themselves, would be forced to answer the why question with this answer, "We do groups so our church grows numerically." While numeric growth is a marker of organizational success, it may not be an indicator that the making of mature disciples is taking place.

The first step in developing a healthy group culture in your church is to develop a strategy that governs your disciple-making process for the church as a whole. In order for this to gain traction, you must be clear on your "why." Your "why" should be a theological strategy and not a pragmatic strategy. A pragmatic strategy would be to increase attendance. A theological strategy would be to care for the church of God through the shepherding of a flock (Acts 20:28; 1 Pet. 5:1–4).

The second step in developing a disciple-making strategy is creating a plan. This would seem obvious, but many churches do not have a plan at all. When asked, "Does your church have an intentional plan for discipling individuals in your congregation and encouraging their spiritual growth?" about four in five Protestant pastors said yes.[4] Of the churches surveyed, 21 percent do not have an intentional plan for spiritual growth. (And, between us, a lot of people answer that they have a plan, but when you dig deeper, it's not really a plan but is more like an idea.)

For those pastors with an intentional plan, the majority (56%) says the first priority in their plan is focused on biblical knowledge. The other options given—relationship and encouragement focused

(21%), equipping and how-to focused (11%), experience or service focused (9%)—are prioritized by a smaller number of churches.

While having a plan is a critical second step, evaluating the results is equally important. Only 43 percent of the pastors surveyed said their church regularly evaluates discipleship progress among their congregation, but they do believe progress is being made. Over 90 percent of pastors agree their congregation is making significant progress in their spiritual development, but less than half are satisfied with the state of discipleship and spiritual formation in their church. This would indicate that pastors are probably looking for improvement but have rarely had anything measurable to determine what or how much progress is truly being made.

In other words, many feel good about it but don't really know why!

From Monologue to Dialogue

When we talk about groups—regardless of size, purpose, and meeting place—we are talking about a smaller setting where people move from sitting in rows to actually sitting in circles. At that point the group transitions from monologue to dialogue, and things get really personal in a transformational way.

With the right group values, leaders, and environments, a supernatural process of discipleship happens. The potential for the multiplication of disciples and groups becomes greater. Disciples engage in community where they're dealing with issues of church, ministry, and mission.

At LifeWay Research, we're passionate about the state of the church. And the overwhelming statistical evidence supports that healthy churches have people meeting in smaller groups. In those groups they are growing together in community with Christ and one another as they become more effective in God's mission.

At the same time we see an unsettling deficit of disciple making in the church today. And a lot of that has to do with the fact that people are not in smaller groups or communities. We surveyed thirty-five hundred American and Canadian churchgoers, in English, Spanish, and French.

Here's what we found: less than half sacrifice their own desires to provide for those in need. And typically people overstate their engagement in good things and understate their engagement in bad things when asked those types of survey questions. We are all like that, aren't we?

Over a third of the people we surveyed never exercise their spiritual gifts to serve God and others. And Bible engagement is the most telling statistic because it correlates most clearly to all other areas of growth. Only 19 percent of churchgoers read their Bible every day. This is an important statistic to remember as the group begins to dialogue about a book that 81 percent do not read daily.

The church has a discipleship deficit. Now for some the answer is to have more exciting worship. For others it's to have more exciting programs. Both can be helpful and life giving. But phrases like, "It's all about the weekend" come out of a "weekend warrior" approach to disciple making. At best, in too many large churches that are succeeding at attracting crowds, there is more of a mass evangelism outcome versus making world-impacting disciples who live out the Great Commission. This mind-set occurs gradually with growing churches and is rarely the stated intention.

So a dynamic communicator and wonderful music may gather a crowd, but if people never move from sitting in rows to sitting in circles, the gospel impact will be insignificant. People gathering in classrooms to get great information delivered by superstars like Beth Moore and Tim Keller may grow in knowledge—and we are thankful for both—but the end result is that we end up in a discipleship deficit if monologue does not transition to meaningful dialogue.

One of the keys in the discipleship process is the issue of transformational groups. If you're counting, the New Testament has more than thirty "one anothers" that cannot be lived out in weekend services. In other words, the New Testament gives more than thirty "one another" commands that you can't do sitting in a row next to some-one at church.

That's the difference between proximity and community, between location and living.

You can sit next to people every week and be in proximity to them. You sit close but remain strangers. The best churches, how-ever, help people move from proximity to community. They help more people from sitting close to being close, by moving people from sitting in rows to sitting in circles. Those churches transition people from having a similar location to doing life together. They move them from seeing one another to doing the "one anothers" of Scripture.

If you are one of those "I hate church people" folks, note that the "one anothers" are addressed to how Christians relate to Christians. Unfortunately, a relational ethic among believers is often ignored to the shame of the gospel. But relationships among Christians are often messier than relationships with lost people. There is a reason the Gospel of John records these words of Jesus: "By this all people will know that you are My disciples, if you have love for one another" (John 13:35).

That takes moving from proximity to community.

Discipleship Methodology

Whether you use home groups, like our churches do, or you have Bible study classes that meet on Sunday morning at your church facility, our research can help inform your strategy. Both small-group approaches, and most other group strategies, support our passion. Groups are more than a methodological choice; they are a biblical mandate and a core practice for transformation.

Some people think they have discovered the "holy grail" of groups, with an attitude that the "best way to do groups is our way." We are not those guys. Methodological snobbery in groups and other fields is too prevalent in the church. Christian leaders become dangerous when they discover something that "works," think every other approach is bad, and want to get you to do exactly what they have discovered.

So we won't tell you where your groups should meet, when your groups should meet, or the exact focus of your groups. We see nothing beneficial resulting from methodological snobbery. Wherever the Word of God is given the authority to speak, the Holy Spirit is allowed to lead and teach, and Jesus' story, the gospel, intersects with and transforms the stories of all involved, spiritual growth will be experienced.

Do we believe effective groups will help churches take consumers and move them from rows to circles, putting them in a better position to become more like Jesus? Absolutely! And although groups are not the only place transformation happens, we are convinced it is the primary place.

We think, as with Jesus' original disciples, that transformational discipleship is not merely rabbinical monologues but includes robust dialogues. Consider the picture Scripture paints of Jesus' dialogue with the disciples: "Who do you say that I am?" (Matt. 16:15) and "You don't want to go away too, do you?" (John 6:67) are more transformational than simple rhetorical questions. These questions from Jesus engaged people who followed Him on a soul level.

People enter the sphere of influence of a local church through multiple points. And when they enter, they are all over the map spiritually. Therefore, it is vital for churches to provide a clear target explaining the attitudes and behaviors of a disciple; you must have a clear definition of *disciple*.

Could you imagine yourself starting a manufacturing business you believe will change your financial future and the generations following you forever? As you begin to build your team and start casting the vision, excitement builds. People sign on. But one day the conversations on your team become a bit awkward. Everyone who signed on forgot to ask a critical question. Someone courageously and nervously blurts out to you:

What are we making?

You calm your nervous team members with a chuckle and reply: "That's easy. We are making widgets. And we are not making ordinary widgets. We are making the greatest widgets the world has ever known." The team, with a great sense of relief, cheers in support and gets back to work.

But a few days later the tension reenters the room as the team members discuss the work. Days of pondering and side conversations have begun to cause another legitimate concern to bubble to the surface. Finally the ice is broken when someone on the team asks the boss:

What's a widget?

Do you see the correlation to the church? You can see why we need to clearly communicate the goal of the most sacred work in history and eternity—disciple making (Matt. 28:19–20).

Your response to the challenge of defining a disciple may be, "Come on, guys, the definition of *disciple* is easy. Everybody knows what a disciple is. . . ." Well, OK, so use the space below to write your definition. But keep in mind you are trying to write something you can clearly identify and measure, so include the attitudes and behavior of a disciple. Yes, you get partial credit (barely) for saying, "A disciple is a Christ follower." But how do you measure that? Baptisms? Small-group attendance? Worship attendance? Giving?

A disciple is . . .

_____

_____

_____

_____

This is not as easy as it looks and has nothing to do with fancy wording. If your discipleship target is really clear, you will begin to say no to more good things than ever before, recognizing that often good things interfere in accomplishing the best thing.

You will also see how groups compliment the mission of the church and cannot possibly stand alone. But every church will struggle with making the mission of God happen in the world if they cannot clearly agree on what the disciple-making mission of God actually looks like.

Groups Matter

Most everybody knows that groups, smaller contexts, and smaller communities are necessary. One of the assumptions you'll find in all the research is that in any effective church life will always include groups that work. But what does work mean, and what's happening to make them work?

Our research revealed that 63 percent of pastors surveyed indicated that they're not satisfied with the state of discipleship in their church. We were not surprised. The question is whether discipleship is the real issue, or is it just the perception of pastors?

When we did *Transformational Church* (TC), the first research project in this series, we studied seven thousand churches from different Protestant denominations, and we found two things. First, pastors weren't assessing the state of their own discipleship. Quality control often takes a backseat to quantitative measurement. And the frustrating part of disciple making is that we all struggle to find satisfactory measurements. So we are not necessarily demonizing pastors about something that is not easy to measure beyond "How many?" and "How much?" Often quantitative measurement is the best we can do.

The second consistent element that emerged from our TC research was that people were generally dissatisfied about the state of the discipleship in their church. So pastors were somewhat oblivious to whether real discipleship was happening in their church, while at the same time people in their churches noticed discipleship was not going well. This disparity is not uncommon.

We want a sense of dissatisfaction in our churches to a certain degree. But there is a perception that the elephant in the room (evangelicalism and beyond) is the lack of robust disciple making in our churches. We think that perception is accurate. We think our research validates that that perception is accurate. A focus on disciple making is critical for the future of life and ministry in the church. It is important to start now to take strategic steps to make advancements in the disciple-making process.

All about Us

Do you think it's possible for a Christian to grow apart from community? We don't. Disciples can't be fully formed apart from community. Community is sanctifying. Blind spots will remain in our lives unless we allow those we trust to look closely at us and tell us exactly what they are seeing. Unfortunately, these people cannot look closely unless they are spending considerable time with us— like in a smaller group of some kind.

The writer of Hebrews spoke to community:

> And let us be concerned about one another in order to
> promote love and good works, not staying away from our
> meetings, as some habitually do, but encouraging each
> other, and all the more as you see the day drawing near.
> (Heb. 10:24–25)

As the basics of life with Jesus were being taught, the importance of life together was an integral part. The Jewish recipients of this letter were caught between the choice of moving forward with Jesus Christ or going backward to their former religious ways. The word according to God was for them to move forward with Christ, together. The writer of Hebrews summoned the followers of Christ to make a decisive change in their habits and their commitment to one another.

This familiar Hebrews passage had a community address. "Let us" was vitally important to context. Christianity has been a "let us" proposition from the calling of the first disciples until today. In this passage we see three different challenges to "us":

1. "*Let us* draw near with a true heart in full assurance of faith" (Heb. 10:22).
2. "*Let us* hold on to the confession of our hope without wavering" (Heb. 10:23).
3. "*Let us* be concerned about one another" (Heb. 10:24).

Our greatest potential to grow in Christ is realized in community—in "us." Readers were asked to "consider" the way to bring out the best in people around them who were following Jesus. The idea was to "take a closer look" and imagine the possibilities of helping someone in their walk with Christ.

What the Hebrews were called to consider is how to "promote" or "provoke" (KJV) "love and good works." The original word for "promote" is an unusual choice—the KJV actually reflects more the meaning of poking, prodding, or irritating someone—to love and serve more. That may sound perversely fun to "aggravate someone to Jesus." But don't forget that whatever we do to irritate others to do, they are to do it right back to us. This only works in community with those we have a relationship with.

We are not sure of the full intent of the passage, but we can relate to the challenge of it. In order for us to personally value groups, we must fight through traffic after a day at work, only to rush through dinner and take care of our children, so that we can spend the evening with our group. As much as we promote groups for spiritual growth, we are not suggesting it is an easy choice. In fact, some days it is just plain irritating. But we need our community, and our community needs us.

No matter how idealistic "life together" might be, we are going to spend an evening with people who are not like us. Prayer requests can go on forever. At times other members are strongly opinionated (but never us!), which causes our Bible discussion to range from the virgin birth to Mormonism to gun control and back. A group commits to one another at all times, not just when it meets our approval.

Here's the reality: if it were up to us, in our sinful flesh, we would never be consistent in meeting together, serving together, and encouraging others to do the same. But an accountability factor moves us beyond what we could normally do and be for God.

We are accountable to others in community. When we think about skipping the next service opportunity or group meeting, we are reminded that they are people just like us, in spite of the fact that they are not like us. If they can serve and meet, so can we. They have the same challenges to get to group that we have, some of them even more. And they have to listen to us rant and whine about our kids' schools, health care reform, and the Buffalo Bills or Miami Heat. As we experience accountability in community, we see a picture of the ultimate source of our real accountability—God Himself. As fellow companions of the Messiah, we watch out for one another's spiritual condition:

> Watch out, brothers, so that there won't be in any of you an evil, unbelieving heart that departs from the living God. But encourage each other daily, while it is still called today, so that none of you is hardened by sin's deception. For we have become companions of the Messiah if we hold firmly until the end the reality that we had at the start. (Heb. 3:12–14)

But as difficult as it is, we just can't stay away from our meetings. As easy as it would be, our spiritual life and health depend on community. And Hebrews 10:24–25 is not just about the prodding, irritating nature of relationships. Community offers something else we need—encouragement to live in the freedom we have in Christ.

Encouragement, unfortunately, is a lacking characteristic of the church. We do not seem to have enough of it. Groups encourage others with hope in Christ in spite of our circumstances. Paul said in 2 Timothy 3:1, "But know this: Difficult times will come in the last days." We need one another!

Martin Seligaman's research in the 1960s on "learned helplessness" is still widely respected among psychologists. Seligaman and his team placed a dog in a cage designed to receive electric shocks. When they hit the cage with a jolt of electricity, the dog jumped and yelped as expected. They waited a few minutes and shocked the cage again, and the dog repeated the jumping and yelping. But after several shocks something strange happened: the dog responded less and less as he was hardened to the impact of the shock.

The researchers opened the door to the cage and shocked the dog, hypothesizing that the dog would leave the cage when he was shocked. But the dog stayed in the cage; he was numb to the pain. He had learned to live helpless, learned to live in captivity even though he was free.

The researchers continued their experiment by involving another dog, a dog not hardened by the electric shock. After being jolted with a shock of electricity, the new dog jumped and yelped as he ran quickly out of the cage. The first dog, seeing there was a better way, followed to the freedom that was already his.

In the same way sin hardens us and deceives us. It causes us to stay in the cage though the door has been opened, though Christ has set us free. We desperately need others around us to encourage us to walk in the freedom Christ has already given us. The writer of Hebrews says, "Encourage each other daily, while it is still called today, so that none of you is hardened by sin's deception" (Heb. 3:13). Community with other believers keeps our hearts tender and soft before the Lord so that He can mature and shepherd us.

Why must we challenge those in our churches to understand that their faith is deeply communal? Because without community believers will fail to live the freedom Christ has purchased for us.

Paul said, "I know that I will remain and continue with all of you for your progress and joy in the faith, so that, because of me, your confidence may grow in Christ Jesus when I come to you again" (Phil. 1:25–26). Paul recognized his vital role in the believers' progress in their faith. This is the role community plays in our faith.

We're not saying growth doesn't happen apart from community. But we don't think it's possible for formation to fully occur without community. When you look at the idea of church in the original Greek language, you see another example. The New Testament, *ecclesia*, means "called-out ones." I'm not just a called "one," but I am part of a *we* and an *us*. We're called-out "ones."

If you do discipleship alone, your spiritual development is slower at best and warped at worst. You might understand some biblical truth. But so much of Scripture has a relational description like "honor one another," "love one another," etc. The entire second half of Ephesians is all about community. So it seems that spending discipleship time alone is like spending time in the first half of Ephesians. You get the theological basis but not the relational basis.

In many contexts we've interpreted growth through the lens of a classroom model, based on knowledge and completing a course of study. For transformation the culture in our churches must shift from mere classroom to community, a community that learns and processes God's Word together and encourages one another to live what they have learned. Learning is not only knowledge gained; it is truth lived out in the context of and under the watch care of a community of Christ followers.

Our research revealed a stark contrast between the spiritual maturity of those who are in community and those who are not. Although we admit that group life is only one of the variables that influence people's growth, there is a significant difference between those who attend group and those who do not.

Competing Systems

Competing systems emerge in a church when no clear vision is consistently cast. Then each ministry, etc., must decide for themselves what they are supposed to do and to what end. We all are clear on the fact that the platform and the lead pastor are a significant part of overall vision casting. But that alone will not fill in all the gaps.

Informal conversations with staff and key leaders must always go back to the "why" of the church. If not, silos will dominate, and tension will always be just below the surface. One of these competing areas can be between weekend services and groups. Because pastors are equippers and they're equipping on Sundays, you can't separate preaching from discipleship. Are some pastors guilty of overvaluing their sermons and undervaluing community? Yes.

At Grace Church, where I (Ed) serve, one of our team members challenged us by pointing out that we're putting a lot of energy into Sunday morning, and yet that is not what we claim to value. We value life change, which is only going to take place on any significant level in community. How do we increase that?

Most would agree that if we have a discipleship deficit, part of the answer is going to be biblical preaching. But what you will find is that most churches put significant energy in biblical preaching on the weekends and have little energy left over for something we believe is equally important—biblical community. Biblical preaching and biblical community are complementary discipleship platforms. We don't have the luxury to choose one or the other. We made a choice to let both important functions of the church feed each other rather than compete with each other.

Our concern is that pastors and leaders seem to miss the connection between group life and spiritual growth. This is a mystery to us for the most part. The radical difference between those in groups and those who are not may be taken for granted.

Let me illustrate. I (Ed) used to play competitive chess in high school. (Yes, I was/am a nerd.) But the illustration may help you, so mock me later. When you play chess, you have to learn how to use all your pieces when most people get reliant on the powerful queen. (The queen can go just about every direction and is the most powerful piece on the board.)

How do you learn how to use all the pieces? Well, you practice without the queen. When you start playing without the queen, you get used to seeing the power of the rook, knight, bishop, and even the pawns.

Here's the point: in most churches where this book will be read, your worship service is the queen. It is what has the power to draw guests. The music attracts. The preaching inspires. And the other pieces, the ones that often have greater lifelong impact (like a long-term, accountable relationship with a brother or sister in Christ), can get underused because the queen has disempowered the rest.

Most of us can only do one thing well—weekends. And yet many players left on the board could make all the difference. So you might have to put less energy into your worship service to empower the rest—or maybe find some new energy. This is counterintuitive to most pastors and Christians.

Now don't misunderstand. We believe in biblical preaching and God-centered worship, but if they don't connect to biblical community, something is missing. It's not working. And it needs to change. This was hard to do at first, but we made that change, and it led to more and deeper disciples.

When I (Eric) consult with churches who have often heard the phrase, "It is all about the weekend," I encourage them to strategically consider, "It's all about the weekend. Then what?"

We want great weekend worship services, and we want them to be transformational. The point is not to ignore weekends and go totally organic, hoping the right things will pop up at the right time. God cares about the weekends and so do we. No matter how hard we try to change that culture, for now people normally seem to find God through the front door of a Sunday morning worship service. So this opportunity deserves our best.

But if the weekend is everything—if that is the totality of what we do—then we are missing the "making disciples" part of the Great Commission. We may be baptizing, but we aren't teaching anybody very much. Who provokes us to "love and good works" (Heb. 10:24) when we are sitting in proximity but not living in community?

Allow us to reiterate this once again: we don't want to minimize the preaching of Scripture. We all believe in preaching as a mark of a biblical church. But both groups and preaching are supernatural and supernaturally important.

What happens in community is supernatural. Something happens in circles that doesn't happen in rows. And the opposite is true; things that happen in the weekend worship service don't happen in community. We don't want to rank one over the other. They're both supernaturally important and both are transformational. But we were surprised about how little community life seems to be valued by people in the local church whether they are connected to community or not.

Our research revealed that the vast majority of those who are in groups never invite anyone to be a part of their group. There's no intentional strategy to reach out beyond the group. We find the "us four and no more" disposition disturbing. Groups can become another consumer-driven choice for many meeting the needs of the third place of engagement. "That's what we need or want, so now we're done, we can check the box" seems to be the attitude of some in groups.

But in fairness, what is really going on in the lives of those who responded to our research? Groups that exist in a church system— are they responding to a group culture that has been created by staff and key leaders? Is this just a lack of understanding of the importance of community even by those who are in community? Or is it simply indicative of a dysfunctional community that we see this to be so prevalent in the church?

Austin Maxheimer, Life Group director at One Life Church in Evansville, Indiana, discovered a dysfunction in group life that was not obvious at first. "Our groups had become complacent. We were adding groups, and everyone considered them to be a raging success." What else does a groups pastor want, right?

He identified the problem, "They weren't reaching for or actively pursuing the church's stated mission of 'helping people far from God experience Jesus.'" He said his groups were more "affirmation circles" that disconnected from One Life's mission. Everybody understood how important weekends were to the mission, but no one saw groups having a role in making the mission happen. Something had to change.

The result was moving the groups' scorecard beyond multiplication and participation. Now there are two questions and two metrics that drive each group at One Life:

1. Are you helping each other experience Jesus daily?
2. Are you actively helping another group of people experience Jesus?

Immunity to Community

Ed preaches three times a month at Grace Church where he is lead pastor. The three-year-old church in the Nashville area has 60 to 70 percent of their adult attendance in small groups. So for most churches that would be impressive numbers.

Surprisingly, a large number of people at Grace Church simply do not think groups are important for them, and some of them are believers. What's disturbing is that when this happens in any of our churches, their lack of community seeps onto the new believers and defines "normal" behavior for a Christ follower. When believers resist biblical community, it is unhelpful for them, unhelpful for the church, and counterproductive to God's mission. Ironically, those who are not in community are influencing other members of the larger community. Community influence works positively and negatively.

Sociologist Robert Putnam, in his book *Bowling Alone*, talks about a seismic shift in our culture. Bowling leagues used to be a big thing, but today people don't join bowling leagues. They bowl alone. Sadly, some people think it is normal to "bowl alone" in the church.

Many homes don't have front porches anymore; they have back decks. If you live in a cold area, you shovel your driveway, but you don't shovel your walkway, because people don't walk to your door. You drive into your garage and shut the door behind you. This cultural trend, dismissing and deemphasizing community, is now being manifested in the life of the church.

This is one of the ways that the gospel has to be countercultural and another reason churches aren't culturally relevant in every way. We may look similar (in some ways) to the world around us, but our values are radically different. One of those values that we need, but the world may not have, is that of a community that is based on a true Savior.

Culture is going to support the attitude that it's all about you and your family. The gospel gives us a different picture as believers all in one family or household. We must counterculturally say, "You think you don't need community, but you're wrong. Your life and relationship with God will not thrive without community."

When the apostle Paul wrote the believers in Philippi from prison, he told them, "I give thanks to my God for every remembrance of you, always praying with joy for all of you in my every prayer, because of your partnership in the gospel from the first day until now" (Phil. 1:3–5). What does "partnership in the gospel" mean?

The word for "partnership" in the original language is *koinonia*, which expresses participation, not merely association. These believers did not merely show up for church; they lived as the church. They participated in one another's spiritual growth. Participation with one another is much deeper than association with one another.

When we fly on an airplane, we are associated with the people surrounding us. We are on the same flight scheduled to land at the same airport. We experience the same bumps, the same views, and the same food. We arrive at the same gate, at the same time, peruse the same magazine in the seat pocket in front of us, listen to the same announcements, and are greeted by the same flight attendants. But despite having the same experience and being next to one another, we are typically not in community with those around us. We associate but we don't participate. By contrast the flight attendants are generally in community as they together serve the passengers.

We fear many churches are like an airplane. Everyone is headed to the same place and filled with people who associate but who don't participate. We can hear the same announcements, sing the same songs, read the same texts, and arrive and leave at the same times without participating—without being, as Paul stated, "in partnership in the gospel." The staff may experience community with one another and may be, therefore, oblivious to the lack of community among the attenders.

If you are a church leader, don't settle for mere association. Preach and plan for participation. Don't be content to lead an airplane-ride church. A church like this has a lot of passengers, but few are transformed. This requires a community.

In order for participation to happen in your congregation, you must do three things: (1) be involved in or leading a transformational group yourself, (2) be certain stories of transformation through groups are being told during weekend worship services, (3) be the primary promoter of groups to the congregation you lead.

When we see three of the prominent images of the church in the New Testament—a family or household (Gal. 6:10), a body (1 Cor. 12:12), and a bride (Rev. 19:7)—we see something much greater than a group of people on a ride together. Each image gives a powerful picture of how biblical community works.

Real community is ever changing. The first impression of biblical community described as the "bride" gives the impression that it's a one-on-one "just me and Jesus on a honeymoon" thing, right? But when we consider the marriage analogy a bit more, we know a bride does not stay in a one-on-one relationship for long. Marriage might be great if it were one lifelong honeymoon, but it is a community event as well as a community project. Two families are joined together, not simply a bride and groom. In most cases children soon arrive. Good-bye honeymoon. Life is in a constant state of flux for a bride and groom.

As the bride of Christ, the church experiences constant change as well. New members should be joining and becoming involved in what God is doing. Some members may be leaving to follow God's leadership for their family to a new area. Hopefully, others are being called out to serve as full-time missionaries, church planters, or pastors. This flux is part of life as the bride.

When we consider this analogy, we must always keep at the front of our mind that the church is a group—*we* are the bride of Christ. For one of us to stand up on a Sunday and declare boldly during our sermon, "I am the bride of Christ," would be, at the very least, theologically questionable.

Real community is learned and discovered. *Family* and *body* seem more communal in nature, but our most natural instincts still avoid accountability and responsibility. Groups normally take time to become community with one another. That is why classrooms or courses are not conducive for community. The content focus and goal of finishing the class makes biblical community unlikely.

Body is something Christians are a part of that is much bigger and more diverse than individuals. When we surveyed people about their personal experience for groups, many of them noted that the diversity of their groups was a major adjustment for them. However, if you are really part of a body, you can't exist outside your role. Just as my physical body has a lot of diversity for its proper functioning, so does the body of Christ; and as such, members of the group need diversity.

Family says I'm part of something important that requires something from me. We think people long for that. People aren't looking for a friendly church; they're looking for friends. But they're still looking generally for superficial friends. You have to lead people into an understanding of real community, and that happens as someone courageously sets aside the natural instinct to remain anonymous, joins a group, and experiences Christian community. Simply teaching about Christian community will never make it possible for someone to understand what Christian community is.

Real community is interdependent. We have a tendency to swing the pendulum away from interdependence to either one of two extremes. We can go to independence, which is what seems to be happening in Western culture in the era of streaming movies and home delivery. We value independence in our context. Virtually every business slogan appeals to your desire to assert your independence and "have it your way," to use just one example. Many think if you're going to be a real man, you're going to be an independent man. Culture says a real woman needs no outside help. You are on your own so "be well fed."

The other side is dependence. For some, your spiritual life is about getting help from your group. The group has become your idol, and you have no real relationship with God apart from group life. Others may have a sense of codependence when life is one big rescue mission for you. Your self-esteem is based on your ability to fix and/or rescue people.

Dietrich Bonhoeffer warned of the extremes:

One who wants fellowship without solitude plunges into the void of words and feelings, and the one who seeks solitude without fellowship perishes in the abyss of vanity, self-infatuation and despair.[5]

We need community. But we often radically swing between independence and dependence. In our case just ask our wives. We don't get sick much, but when we do, the whole world stops. Thus we illustrate our point with the radical swing from independence to dependence as men.

Independence has a dark side that says, "I can do life alone. I can solve all my problems. I don't need outside help." And dependence has a dark side, as well: "I can depend on [my idols] to provide for me instead of God." Both isolation and idolatry grieve God.

Dependent believers prove their spiritual immaturity. Like a newborn babe they cry out through attitudes and actions for everyone else to meet their needs. Independent believers prove they too are not yet spiritually mature. Like many teenagers they tell everyone, "I don't need you. I can do anything I need done without anyone's assistance." The spiritually maturing person on the other hand is interdependent. The interdependent person realizes they need others and others need them and this is a healthy, mature way to live life and grow to spiritual maturity.

We want to lead our people to real biblical community that is neither dependence nor independence. It's interdependence, like a body working together with diverse roles and strengths. Like a family with mutual love and responsibility between each member. And like a bride who is always giving love for and ever receiving love from her husband and children.

Community on Purpose

This issue of independence is often not as prominent in other parts of the world because community is viewed differently in other cultures. Churches like Victory Fort in Metro-Manila (www.victory-fort.org), led by lead pastor Joey Bonifacio, place all their focus on community as the best environment for disciple making and have had incredible results. Victory Fort is a campus of Victory Church (60,000 weekend attenders).

Joey's book, *The LEGO Principle*, is a must-read. His thesis is simple, "Just like LEGO pieces that connect at the top and at the bottom, discipleship is about connecting to God and with one another. This is the LEGO Principle: Connect first to God and then to one another."[6]

Fort in Metro-Manila is only one of many churches in the world that has seen incredible success in and through their groups ministry. But is it a cultural phenomenon? Or is it biblical? Our answer is that it is both.

What happens in the U.S. may not be an exact replica of what happens in West Africa, Australia, Brazil, or the Philippines. Biblical community will be expressed differently in different contexts, both locally and globally. So biblical community will be expressed culturally or counterculturally depending on exactly where you live. If disciple making is the goal of intentional community, inevitably you will face roadblocks, and many of them will be cultural forces.

One of the reasons we don't see biblical community in the church is because we don't understand community as a culture. In West Africa, for example, they often live way out in the bush, in a village. In that environment you see children being raised by other people in the village, just as sort of a natural phenomenon. Yes, in Africa they say it takes a village, and we agree with slight modification outside of the village—it takes a community.

When you go into West Africa and you say, "We need to have community," no real mind-set shift or behavioral changes are needed to make it happen. Yet, in most of the Western world and even among those who are "churched," when you say the same thing, people experience an enormous disconnect.

But it's a biblical mandate for disciple making to flourish in every culture. So how do we realize a biblical and contextualized disciple-making community?

Here are five ways church leadership can be intentional about overcoming cultural barriers to biblical community:

1. Live Community

Pastors need community. In some situations pastors have to lead the first groups in a new church. But set a goal to work yourself out of a job. You can't possibly afford pastors to lead as many groups as you're going to need, no matter how large your church grows. And the best value all pastoral staff members can model is their own need to be in community. From a leadership perspective the biblical role of staff members is to "equip the saints." But there should be a place where staff can practice "being a saint."

Many times pastors, staff, and families think that being in community is too risky. Fear drives them into hiding or to creating "staff only" type groups. Staff-only groups can actually be much more risky than groups with everyday people. Staff members have so many competing agendas, including where everybody belongs on the organizational chart. You can tell your secrets in a staff group, but you always worry they may hurt you in the long term.

At the end of the day, in spite of the risks, do life with your people. They need to see you struggle and process your day-to-day walk with Christ. They need to see you desire community, and you need to see transformation take place among your community.

2. Learn Community

We did not know for sure where this fits. Does a leader need to learn community first or live community first? The best way to learn community is to first live it. We used to be experts on the technical aspects of community and trumpet it from our pulpits, but as we lived it, we were much better at communicating the principles. As we lived and learned what we had been communicating, community became an actual value versus an aspired value.

Study other group models and read books by people who love and value community. They might be books about small groups or even house churches, but be diligent to ask how you can live community in your context. Be a learner—a student—of community.

3. Teach and Preach Community

In most places community doesn't happen accidentally. Your church members will have to learn the meaning of community. Each year at least one sermon series needs to address biblical community. Personal stories about community should be included in the pastor's sermons year-round as well as through informal conversations. Yet before any of these shifts happen, leaders must have clarity about the meaning of community and be highly motivated to make it a priority. One church with more than five hundred groups invites people at the end of every service to join a group. They have a Groups Concierge counter prominently set in the foyer to help people find a group. Group leaders stand in the foyer and find people who are not in community, and they invite them to join a group. Groups won't just happen organically. The process of groups needs to be tilled, planted, watered, and nurtured before it can reap a harvest.

You have to teach it, herald it, and live it.

4. Create Heroes from and for the Community

People realize what you long for them to do and become when they have heroes to look up to. And, in order for there to be heroes of community, you must create them. During your sermons tell the stories of people who were hesitant to get into a group but have had significant life change in a group. At the end of the story, tell the congregation how proud you are of the person this story was about. Another way to raise up heroes is to do a short video interview with someone who has joined a group and is journeying significantly with others. Do whatever it takes to make heroes of those who have joined a group and are being transformed. As you raise up heroes, you will also be telling everyone else what they can and should strive to become.

5. Celebrate Community

When your people think you are teaching, advertising, and inviting people into community too much, you are almost there. *Teach, advertise, and invite more.* And remember, you are not only celebrating to educate and invite but also to cast vision for new leaders to step forward. People are drawn toward what seems most important to the church. And no matter how many groups you have, a healthy church will never have enough.'

From the Group

I am able to do life with ten to fifteen other Christians. We are able to worship, pray, talk about Jesus, and support one another. All this for the mission and plan that God has for each one of us.

—Tom

What Now?

- What is your definition of a disciple?
- How do you plan to make disciples as a church?

4
Integration

LeaderSpeak

Contrary to Western evangelicalism's obsession with the individual, discipleship is and always was a group project. No one in the New Testament followed independent of other followers.
—Steve Murrell, *Wikichurch*

Next Step: *Identify the kind of group to support your church's disciple-making mission.*

Andrew and Laura Lynn had perfectly good reasons not to try one of their church's groups. Andrew's new job as tennis coach at a local university necessitated their move to a new city. As a young couple they knew this would be one in a series of moves necessary at their phase in life. The multiple demands of campus life as well as the feeling of being temporary in the community made trying a group seem low on their priority list.

Andrew admitted his concerns, "I think our biggest apprehension was the time commitment. We really did not want to commit to something we were going to have to bail out of eventually." Andrew's concerns are common among people who are thinking about group life. Making a decision to add a commitment to an already overcommitted schedule is a perfectly good reason to "just say no." It seemed even worse to commit and then back out once it got going.

Time and commitment were not the only concerns stopping them from trying a group. "Subconsciously, you are always worried if you should let others in your life," Andrew said. "What are they going to do with that? What is it going to look like?" Laura Lynn agreed with Andrew and added, "We were scared to get really committed and involved with a group of people." Common concerns of new group attenders include fear of being put on the spot and worries about really fitting in.

Trying a group can be a huge step of faith, and concerns about that step are real, but Andrew and Laura Lynn took the risk. Groups are a great place to find new friends and develop a deeper faith in God. It might even surprise some participants how much they have been missing this from their life.

Although going to a group has involved a new commitment, the payoff in their relationship with God and others has been worth it. "If you step out in faith, God is going to do great things in your life," Andrew said. "Our apprehensions were totally taken away once we started."

Laura Lynn described her discovery of "real people just like you doing life together." She loves the friendship, encouragement, and support she has enjoyed from her group. She is learning that other people have had the same struggles she did. She thought she was the only one who doubted God, that is, until she started really talking with people in her group.

Over time the steps of faith continued for Andrew and Laura Lynn. Their group mission focused on the poorest neighborhood in their city. They engaged people with the gospel that lived without water or electricity, giving time and personal resources. They quickly grew into leading their own group of young professionals and college students as well as serving in other areas of the church.

Although it may seem that these were natural next steps for someone growing in Christ, the independent variable was the group. Not only did Andrew and Laura Lynn find a new platform for gospel-focused mission; they also found another way to take their influence to other levels as group leaders. And because of the way groups were integrated into the mission of their church, they became champions of the mission, not merely group champions.

Groups almost always become inherently more valuable to God's mission of transformation and mobilization when they fit somewhere in a local church. Groups that attempt to operate independently from the church vision and mission can lack focus. They often get focused on niche issues and miss out on other foundational aspects of group life.

Defining *integration* is important to this step in laying the foundation for groups:

Integration—behavior, as of an individual, that is in harmony with the environment.[1]

Integration will not naturally take place in your average local church—it requires intentionality. A plethora of agendas, passions, and ministries make most churches look like a methodological circus or a political convention. Chaos exists and marginalizes the real mission God has given the church. The principle of integration includes groups but has multiple applications no matter what part of the circus you are trying to tame.

Harmony is such a beautiful word. You may think it is idealistic, but what realistic options do you prefer? The opposite of harmony is chaos. Don't settle for this. Way too much is at stake. Integration is the key to harmony in a church.

In 1971, Coca-Cola released one of the most famous television commercials in history. The advertisement—which, if you are too young to remember is on YouTube—featured teenagers from all over the world singing, "I'd like to teach the world to sing in perfect harmony." Although the song did not produce perfect harmony, it sure captured the attention of the world for quite some time.

Imagine if everything in your church worked in harmony for the same purpose. Should that be so idealistic in a church God owns? How can you create that kind of environment? How can you invite God into the process? How can you bring peace to chaotic relationships and systems that break down?

Groups that Work

Groups are composed of different types of people. Age, sex, marital status, or interests can define a group. Other groups represent a cross-section of all of the above, which again, defines the group. Groups can be developed for a variety of purposes. But the effectiveness of a group is in direct proportion to the support, encouragement, and empowerment of church leaders. If leaders see a group as just another program, it becomes a competing system that is marginalized and rendered less effective.

The primary reason most group ministries aren't working is due to the fact that church leaders are oftentimes most passionate about running programs. They see as their role to run efficient programs rather than to make mature disciples. They get their sense of worth when a large crowd shows up for an event, a committee meeting runs smoothly, or the finance team gives them a much greater budget than they had last year. In order for groups to become transformational and the gospel to infiltrate the hearts of group members and ultimately transform them into the likeness of Christ, church leaders are going to have to redirect their focus of attention from the oversight of programs to the transformation of individual people.

Nearly all pastors surveyed (97% including 71% strongly) agree that small classes or groups are very important at their church. It is easy to say something is important, but it is another thing altogether to demonstrate its importance. In a follow-up question, pastors emphasized the importance through their involvement. Once again 97 percent agreed (74% strongly) that their church leadership is personally involved in small classes.

In a survey among Protestant pastors, 76 percent agree (32% strongly) that groups are the primary network to mobilize their church and its work. Therefore, churches expect to use these groups to have an impact in their church and community. When it comes to the type of impact, pastors were asked to select the most valued outcome among four different possibilities.

- Existing individuals following Christ more closely   50%
- More new individuals included and hearing the gospel 20%
- Existing members growing closer to each other   18%
- More individuals outside the church being served   8%

This shows us that pastors place much value on seeing their current attendees increase in the walk with Christ. Andrew and Laura Lynn's story serves as an example of at least three out of four of the above categories: follow Christ more closely, existing members growing closer, and more individuals served.

Pastors were asked about specific activities that could occur within a group. They could select as many activities as possible, and many did. Of the eight activities listed, 35 percent of pastors selected all of them, and nearly three-fourths selected at least six. The following table shows the percentage of pastors who selected each of the activities.

- Bible study   97%
- Prayer   95%
- Care for those in the class or group   85%
- Inviting people to their class or group   79%
- Socializing during regular meetings   78%
- Socializing and events outside the regular meetings 68%
- Service to those outside the church   65%
- Follow-up with visitors to the church   60%

While we would all agree that each of these activities is important, are groups able to accomplish each activity effectively? One can imagine a group that greatly enjoys socializing being less effective in serving those outside the church. A group that enjoys Bible study may not be the most effective in inviting people to their class or group.

Remember the outcome options and the responses by pastors? A similar question was asked of those currently attending groups. The attendees were asked to rank the four different outcomes with the most important outcome receiving a value of one and the least important a value of four. Here is the average ranking of the different outcomes (most important to least important):

- Existing individuals following Christ more closely   1.78
- Existing members growing closer to each other   2.50
- More new individuals included and hearing the gospel   2.61
- More individuals outside the church being served   3.11

These results are similar to what we saw with the pastors. Additionally, nonattenders ranked the four outcomes in the same order. Is it possible for a single group to simultaneously achieve all of the outcomes at the same level? Our research indicates *no*. Do leadership qualities align themselves with different outcomes? Our research indicates *yes*.

So what must lead pastors and group pastors decide next?

Know the purpose of your groups. The data tells us that different aspects of groups (including when, where, and leadership attributes) can be aligned with different outcomes. As you discover your church's disciple-making strategy, then determine what kind of group best supports that overall vision. This brings harmony to your disciple-making process.

Determine the purpose(s) for your groups, and stick to it. Church leaders must know how groups fit into their overall discipleship strategy and process, but many don't. They simply have groups because that is what churches do. Once leaders know where groups fit, the next step is to equip, empower, and release leaders in alignment with the disciple-making mission of the church.

According to the research, the most effective groups were the most focused. People who attended groups that understood the primary purpose of their groups reported a higher level of group effectiveness. Those who attended groups in churches with a plethora of purposes had less effective groups. Groups that are crystal clear as to why they meet and how they fit into the overall life of the church are more effective.

Groups that gather with an attempt to be everything don't accomplish much of anything. For example, a group that attempts to constantly invite unbelievers while simultaneously teaching the Bible in depth, with the hopes of connecting believers together in deep relationships, while living on mission together in the community sounds like a great group. If you are a lead pastor or groups pastor, you might say, "That's exactly the kind of group I want at my church."

This group model has saturated the groups movement. And, while it may seem to be the perfect model for a church achieving all of its goals—especially those churches that do groups, worship, and youth and children's ministry only—it is humanly impossible for a group and a group leader to be and do all of these things. For one thing, group leaders are going to be passionate primarily about one, not all of the things just mentioned. For this reason they will give the majority of their attention to that which they are most passionate about and will feel guilty and ineffective for not accomplishing the rest. Time constraints are also a concern. Asking a nonstaff member to prepare and teach an in-depth Bible study weekly, meet the emotional needs of group members, oversee ongoing missional experiences, and disciple every group member is like asking grass to stop growing in the spring. You're asking the impossible. The average person just doesn't have that kind of time.

But that group is impossible. According to the research the lack of focus is a detriment to their overall effectiveness. To identify the chief purpose (or two purposes) that groups exist at your church and then focus energy in that direction is more effective.

So, as you think about your groups, what are the primary reason(s) you have them? It may be helpful to force rank the list below. In light of your overall church discipleship plan, what are the most important purposes for your groups?

- Formation (teaching and study)
- Connection (connecting believers in biblical community)
- Mission (serving on mission together)
- Invitational (inviting nonbelievers to the group)

You are looking for the primary purpose. You can't pick all of them! What should be your primary purpose? That depends on your overall discipleship strategy. For example, if your weekend worship teaching is forty to forty-five minutes of biblical exposition, your groups may not need to be a duplication of that. You may decide that your groups should carry a different primary purpose. Of course, you would want the groups to study the Scriptures together, but the intended purpose may be connection and community around those studies.

On the other hand, some churches really need their groups to carry the burden of formation and study because the weekend teaching is designed as more of a topical, front-door experience. Choose based on where groups fit in the overall mission of the church as well as what your church currently does well.

The sweet spot is integration of groups into the overall disciple-making mission of the church. They work in harmony with the overall discipleship process. When you surrender your desire for groups to be "all things to all people" (1 Cor. 9:22), then groups become more valuable for the vision of transformation and less of a competing structure. All of the four purposes are biblical and important. The point is that one group cannot effectively do all four. They can focus on one or two and have some involvement in the other, but you need clarity of which ones are the priorities and which are part, but not the focus, of the plan. Your group's effectiveness would be greater if its focus was an augmentation of your weekend services and not duplication. Decide what role each plays in the disciple-making process.

Match leaders with the purpose of your groups. You will read more about this later, but it's important to address this when discussing your approach to groups as well as your intended outcomes. Most churches are desperate for leaders. However, they often hold really high standards and expectations for those leaders. When these highly qualified and motivated leaders can't be found in the congregation, many churches default to lowering their standards to leaders who are willing and available. It's even better if these leaders happen to be aware of their gifts and passion. But we could care less what their gifts and passion are because they are willing and available.

A mind-set shift from leadership needs to happen here regarding the training and selection process. In the short term this may cause progress to go slower than you would like, but long-term integration is much more likely. For groups to be the most powerful, there must be harmony between the purpose of the groups and the leaders who lead the groups.

Leaders should be recruited and trained based on the purpose of the groups. If a church decides the primary purpose of a group is study, then the church should recruit teachers. If a church decides the primary purpose is biblical community, the church should recruit leaders to shepherd and facilitate. If a church decides it is mission, the church should train their leaders to think like missionaries.

Frustration and friction exist if there is not a match. For example, if a church desires the groups to connect people together, but a leader who is recruited wants to teach, things will not go well. Their fifty-two-minute Bible lecture every week complete with charts, graphs, and maps will be painful. The group will lack focus and fail to deliver on the group expectations in light of the overall church discipleship strategy.

Other issues—launching new groups, communication in groups, moving new people to groups, etc.—are also important, but church leaders must first understand how groups fit into the overall discipleship strategy for their church and be zealous about integration. Groups that don't fit . . . don't fit. Not only are they less effective than groups that do fit, but an even greater danger of becoming a competing system is more likely. As you recruit and develop leaders to effectively lead groups with the purpose of your groups in mind, ensure your leaders are encouraged, empowered, and accountable.

Encouraged Leaders

A small group is not an independent franchise but a critical piece of the disciple-making puzzle of your local church. When groups become a competing system within your overall church system, chaos, conflict, and underachieving are sure to follow.

Groups with strong leaders will fill in the gaps if there are no environments for connecting, coaching, and resourcing. They will pick their own studies, form their own structures, and decide their own values. The greatest way to build loyalty to the vision of disciple making is to help group leaders lead their groups! Integrate them into something much bigger than themselves.

The first reality the pastoral staff should understand is what an incredible challenge it is to lead a group every week. This must be put in context of the crazy lives of the group leaders. Many are married with dual careers and multiple children. We have to be careful not to expect them to devote as much time as a staff person.

They get home from work late after a long day. Instead of their normal hurried routine of a quick supper, helping kids with homework, heading off to soccer practice, and running one load of wash through the cycle, something else is done on Tuesday at 7:00 p.m.—small group!

The kitchen must be cleaned, dirty clothes moved into some poor kid's bedroom. One parent goes up to the office bedroom to cram forty-five minutes to an hour in lesson prep while the other prepares coffee, soft drinks, chips and dip. Let the chaos begin.

For some unknown reason the first group attenders arrive at 6:48 when nobody is close to ready so they are awkwardly invited in. Mom makes small talk while she nervously completes the preparation details. The doorbell rings again and another couple arrives. At the same time the group leader's youngest son complains of a stomachache and wants Mom's help with his math homework.

The night ends, well the group part of it anyway, around 9:00 if no one needs to stay late for "prayer or encouragement." The group leaders are then left with helping the kids prepare for the next day inside a cluttered house whose daily chores just got behind schedule for the rest of week. If they are really lucky, they will fall exhausted into bed before midnight.

Before this begins to sound like a "married with children" pity party, we understand problems are not limited to one demographic. There is not a life situation—single, married, divorced, young, old, unemployed, or stay-at-home mom—that does not present incredible obstacles to leading a group well. Many leaders will take shortcuts, not because they are unspiritual but because during most weeks they are in way over their heads.

"But those group leaders just don't get the vision," the groups pastor complains. Maybe not, but you are fortunate that they give so much with so little help. More help could lead to more disciples and group leaders on board with your priorities. If group leaders don't see the vital role groups play in the overall disciple-making strategy, they are ready to quit after three weeks. If they understand the integrated vision, every week is hard but worth it.

Understand this and work to counteract it as much as possible. Keep your leaders connected and encouraged. Celebrate their wins frequently during weekend gatherings. By doing so, you have not only integrated them, but you will also attract others to group involvement and leadership. Provide coaching. Communicate frequently. Buy books that will help them. Teach them to network with one another. Gather them in huddles, but make sure those are high quality and worth another night of the week. Raise leaders of leaders. Let them lead themselves so their next helpful conversation is only one person away from them. Leaders need to be encouraged regularly, and they need to feel as though they have been given the keys and are trusted to lead others.

Empowered Leaders

We are not suggesting you lower the bar because of the busy lives of group leaders. Rules, expectations, and intense training are great; but responsibility and accountability without empowerment lead to burnout or conflict. Raise the bar, but do it alongside giving your leaders all they need to succeed, and you will discover they will lead their groups well.

When you help in this way, your church and the mission of God stand to win big! And when you help them lead their groups well, they will not only embrace their calling on a deeper level; they will embrace the church vision for disciple making.

Their roles are mission critical, and most of them lead on high levels in their vocations and neighborhoods. So lead them as you would expect to be led. Pastoral staff must understand that leading leaders is different from leading followers. We all love them—both leaders and followers, but the conversations are totally different.

Ed coined the term *clergification*, which describes the evolution of a two-class system in the local church.[2] Although the average person may not articulate it that way, a subtle undercurrent bottlenecks ministry in churches. The laity feel unqualified to make decisions or shepherd people. And the clergy is reluctant to trust them to do the same.

Clergy—The group or body of ordained persons in a religion, as distinguished from the laity.[3]

Laity—The body of religious worshipers, as distinguished from the clergy.[4]

Clergy has been a standing designation for the professionally, often seminary trained, people who have expressed a calling from God to lead churches. Throughout the ages clergy have set themselves apart by wearing different clothes (collars and other garb), being highly educated, and even taking certain vows. These elite, specially called groups of leaders are in place because of the inability of a less educated *laity* to hear from God and lead others. The clergy has existed for hundreds of years to do things laity could not do for themselves—or so we are led to believe.

So as it pertains to church leadership in this century, we are calling for a mind-set shift. Although we see value in opportunities like seminary education and believe in being called to specific vocational ministry callings, we do not believe in a class system.

The "declergification" of the church is critical. For congregations to thrive, the priesthood of all believers must not only be taught but also practiced. This is most evident in leading, shepherding, teaching, and counseling members of a group by nonvocational leaders.

Grace Church in Nashville is the church Ed serves. Empowering the laity to lead and pastor people is crucial to their survival because of their current leadership structure—Ed has a full-time job at LifeWay Research and volunteers as the pastor of Grace Church. And for the record, Grace is not a large church (around three hundred on Sunday morning at the time of this writing). If people are going to be pastored at Grace Church, it's going to happen through the organic simplicity of groups. Ed is the pastor, but he doesn't have the ability to personally pastor all the people. As a part-time volunteer, he preaches, leads a group, and leads the staff.

The same happens in larger churches. But this pastoral model is most healthy no matter the size. People can pastor one another so much more effectively than a professional. And this model is more sustainable as the church grows numerically. You can never hire enough professional clergy to meet the real needs of your people. When you start out with empowered laity as group pastor/shepherds, then the DNA of your church is set to be healthy and grow.

Declergification is a biblical principle that moves the focus of ministry where God intended. Group leaders in their discipling role must help Christ followers embrace their biblical identity and role in the mission of God:

> But you are a chosen race, a royal priesthood, a holy nation, a people for His possession, so that you may proclaim the praises of the One who called you out of darkness into His marvelous light. (1 Pet. 2:9)

When we declergify, a critical truth will drive us—the "royal priesthood" of every Christ follower. This truth will move beyond sermon cliché or memory verse to a core value that influences everything.

The word chosen for *priest* in Latin means "bridge builder." Priests build bridges between God and man. Their unique access to God gives them incredible influence in the community. And they leverage that influence to speak for God.

People were in awe of priests in the Old Testament. For leadership as well as the mission of God to work today, pastors need to embrace the "priesthood of the believer." Declergification hits an unfortunate wall if the clergy does not believe in the ability of the "royal priests" God has given them to release. Declergification in your church starts with the clergy. Vocational pastors must view themselves as one of the boys, one of the many priests appointed by God to build bridges for people.

Keep in perspective they are not your everyday priests. They are "royal" or priests fit for a king! The level of angst and mistrust toward people in the pew or padded chair today cannot be understated. And the effort to control and underuse those same people sabotages the mission of God.

Pastors, stand in awe of the people God has entrusted to you. Fall in love with them again, and dream big dreams about how God can use them all over the world. God inspired Peter to identify them as "a chosen race, a royal priesthood, a holy nation, a people for His possession." They are your greatest and most valuable resources other than God Himself.

Pat Hood, pastor of LifePoint Church in Smyrna, Tennessee, is in awe of his people. What God has done at LifePoint over the past ten years is incredible. You can read the amazing story in his book, *The Sending Church: The Church Must Leave the Building.*

This suburban Nashville church experienced a dramatic turning point as a result of a "sacred gathering" season of corporate prayer and fasting. God sent LifePointers out of their building into the community and the nations at an incredible rate. People with six-figure jobs sold everything they had and moved to countries like Belgium and Thailand. Students moved into local, low-income housing projects to live among the poor and marginalized. That is a royal priesthood!

Group leaders need encouragement to persevere faithfully and joyfully, and they need empowerment to do what God allows them to do as a (better) pastor to the people. But they also need to understand how they fit into the overall strategy of the church and take responsibility for their roles.

Accountable Leaders

At Grace Church we ask our group leaders to submit weekly online reports so we know what's going on and that we are hitting the disciple-making target of our church. But at the end of the day, a robust, transformational group system keeps leaders connected, resourced, and accountable.

Submission is a word some people don't like, but it's a helpful one. For harmony to exist, mutual respect and support must also exist. If you find an unwillingness to submit from the group leaders in a reluctance to complete reports or other ongoing communication with staff, that person has a problem submitting and may be the kind of person you don't want in church leadership.

We expect group leaders to be about staying connected and measuring results. Leaders are given the opportunity to submit to the future pastoral ministry team of the local church.

Keep your reporting expectations simple and substantive. Assess each question you ask or each expectation you have. If you do not devour what information your group leaders submit and let their data inform your next steps, you are asking unnecessary questions and just making it harder for them to lead.

Three Seismic Shifts for Integration

I (Ed) like to say that change never happens until the pain of staying the same exceeds the pain of change. Unfortunately this change process is often proceeded by a painful, and at times, substantive moment. For instance, it often seems like people are most willing to listen about spiritual things, when they have a need in their life. Sadly, it often seems like the church waits for difficulty to exist in their community before they respond with service. These seismic moments can be difficult, but can have a silver lining; namely they can be an opportunity for people to see and experience the love of God. Our prayer is that your community does not require a significant and painful moment to see that your church loves them, but we recognize that is may require some substantial shifts in the way you and your people are thinking in order to see your groups become what they need to be.

We're all a kingdom of priests. Pastors, you are simply the leaders of the priests under your care. Your role is to exhort your people in your groups to understand this and become ministers or bridges to God. For this transition to be complete, the local church culture must make three seismic shifts. As the shifts are made, small groups become integrated into the mission of the church, and healthy reproduction can take place. Leaders are encouraged and empowered. More transformed disciples and communities are the result.

Shift 1. From People Called to the Ministry to People Called to Ministry

The word *the* before *ministry* reflects a separatist mind-set between clergy and people. And it is much more than just respecting the pastoral ministry role and assignment.

All of us are called to ministry. Everyone. For groups to be well cared for and for disciples to be made through the groups in a local church, leaders must be viewed as *undershepherds*. Now the obvious question is, under whom? So, are those on the pastoral staff the shepherds? Yes. Then small-group leaders are undershepherds who shepherd under pastors.

Group leaders should not be a group of rogue teachers who pass information on to group attenders and render opinions on the direction of the church. Group leaders play an essential role in the overarching discipleship mission of a local church. They are called to minister.

The pastoral staff has been assigned by God as undershepherds under Christ. The word for *pastor* and *shepherd* are actually the same word in the original Greek. So group leaders are undershepherds. But what we have to recognize is that all of the people we shepherd are called to ministry just as we're called to ministry. Where transformational groups work, group leaders are empowered to step into a higher level of functionality. They function as one called to ministry and are catalysts for others they lead to do the same. We're all called to ministry.

People need to gain more ownership in the church. For some of you, this is an awkward suggestion. People owning the church doesn't necessarily sound like a good thing. Disgruntled churched people who feel entitled to have a voice in every decision in "their church" have been your worst nightmare in the past. And you have lived that nightmare enough to be determined never to live it again.

God bless you. All of us have been there. But that should not cause us to discourage ownership in the church.

Creating environments where people feel more responsible for the outcomes of the church does have a certain degree of risk, but there is more risk in being dependent on a ministerial superman. The reach of the church is limited as long as there is too high a view of the clergy. If the view is that the pastor is the only one who can do certain things, then the pastor will be the only one. And the losers, in addition to the pastor, will be the pastor's family, the church, and the people who refuse to serve.

Another reason some pastors are reluctant to encourage ownership is because of their own visionary leadership. Part of your vision is to lead toward what God wants your church to be and do in the world. Entertaining the possibility of empowering leaders feels like a setback. Their opinions and ideas will slow progress. They need to follow or get out of the way. Again, we understand.

When people take a mature level of spiritual ownership of God's church and mission, everything changes for the better, and all types of greater possibilities exist. The reality is that the people who attend your church are either owners or customers. Would you rather take a chance of keeping the remaining customers and never growing? Or how about mature ownership?

Another reason for reluctance toward ownership is insecurity on the part of the pastor. He may feel his role is not needed in the church if he allows others to lead. And if others lead more effectively, will he be dismissed? In some cases he feels a deep desire to be personally needed by the congregation. This codependent relationship is not biblical and is not healthy.

Ephesians 4 gives an invaluable description of how healthy ministry through the local church should look. Roles and responsibilities are given for specific outcomes. It's the closest thing you have in Scripture to an organizational chart. See this as a picture of God's design team for His mission along with the positions they should play:

And He personally gave some to be apostles, some
prophets, some evangelists, some pastors and teachers, for
the training of the saints in the work of ministry, to build
up the body of Christ. (Eph. 4:11–12)

Jesus gave "people gifts" to His church for specific purposes.
For example, the local church was intended to do evangelism, but
they needed to see the world through the eyes of an evangelist and
be challenged by one. The same would be true of mission expansion and of the forth-telling, clear, moral, and spiritual teaching of a
prophet. All of these lenses are important for the local church. They
give insight, perspective, challenge, and inspiration. None of these
people were necessarily paid professionals. But they were gifted for
specific roles the body of Christ needed.

Then there is the pastor-teacher. The pastor cares for the flock
but also teaches them how to live out faith on a daily basis. Like a real
shepherd, the pastor deals with the day-to-day messes in which the
sheep find themselves. A pastor lovingly, patiently works through
life issues and teaches God's solutions.

We believe small-group leaders are the closest things we have
to the New Testament explanation of what a pastor-teacher does.
When most think of pastor-teacher, they think of someone like Rick
Warren. No question, they're pastor-teachers too.

But the simplicity that marked the early church came from pastor-teachers who were actually local functionaries who led house-
church-type communities. The closest thing that meets this definition
is small-group leaders, not well-known megachurch pastors.

Shift 2. From Exceptional to Ordinary

The leaders in the kingdom of God are ordinary people who
serve in ordinary ways. The power of God rests on them, and they
are more essential to the future of the local church, much more than
the extraordinary people with extraordinary skills.

What are your stated qualifications for group leaders? If you have too many qualifications, you risk eliminating your best. Gifted, qualified leaders serving now can discourage some who may become additional great leaders before they ever become candidates. Ensure that your best leaders are the biggest champions for developing new ones. Your most gifted people need to be training, coaching, and mentoring their replacements.

If your standards are artificially high, lower the standard of organizational leadership, and people will be more likely to lead and participate. Use 1 Timothy 3 as your guide; resist other man-made criteria that turn your small group into a mini-church with Western cultural expectations for professional leaders. One of the most urgent challenges we face is to create a culture in our groups that moves people into leadership, but that carefully watches them grow as they lead.

Sunday morning preaching won't have the same impact on people that group leaders will. The informal Tuesday night conversation can be transformational. When someone says, "You know, I don't really know the Bible very well." The group leader can say, "You know what? I know the Bible only because someone helped me, and I am still learning." But leaders need to use the opportunity to promote the ordinary. People need to be encouraged to know that God uses ordinary people to do ordinary things in extraordinary ways.

Shift 3. From Needing Priests to Being Priests

Every culture in the world creates priests.

Many assume priests were unique to Roman Catholicism, but it's a universal constant in anthropology. If you went to South Africa among the tribal Xhosa, you would find the same thing with different terminology. The same with the Iban in Malaysia. People create religion and then create priests to do their religious work for them.

In some unfortunate circumstances there are Protestants who misunderstand the role of the pastor and who view their pastor as their priest. (We know there are denominations that use the term and get that Martin Luther, for example, was a priest, but the concern here is when a priest replaces the role of the priesthood of believers.)

You see, everyone is tempted to have a priest. Why? Because every culture in the world creates a religious leader whose job is to embody the religious desires of the people. That's human nature, but it's not good for the church today.

God used priests for a season—those who represented people to God and God to people. But the shift of covenants between the old to the new means we no longer need a priest because we're now a kingdom of priests. God predicted this would happen:

> Now if you will listen to Me and carefully keep My
> covenant, you will be My own possession out of all the
> peoples, although all the earth is Mine, and you will be My
> kingdom of priests and My holy nation. (Exod. 19:5–6)

Thus, everyone is a priest who is a follower of Christ. Some of these priests will be leaders of your small groups, and, as such, they will be priests leading priests. And they will do it in many different ways.

As pastor-teachers, group leaders are responsible to use their gifts. But also the pastor-teacher is to help others use their gifts. It is a matter of using what God has given:

> Based on the gift each one has received, use it to serve others,
> as good managers of the varied grace of God. (1 Pet. 4:10)

Give God the opportunity to speak though people as well as through you. Over the years we have been amazed at how God speaks through people in a group. Often those that are the newest in Christ are His best spokespeople. Years of religious opinions and teaching are not built up in their minds. They are not afraid of getting something wrong. So they speak.

There may be times when a group leader has to seek out another pastor to help clarify a theological question, but it should be rare. Group leaders are, in many ways, like the pastors mentioned in the

New Testament. Some churches, in recognizing this, actually call their small group leaders "lay pastors."

What if you were out in a remote area of Africa teaching the Bible and a difficult question came from the group? What would you do then? Pastor-teachers of groups must learn to find answers on their own and teach those in their group to do the same. Ordinary people helping ordinary people find answers—that is what a kingdom of priests does.

If you're going to create a culture of ordinary simplicity in groups, everyone needs to participate. The best answer to a hard question might be, "Let's all go home to study, pray, and find God's answer to this tough question." Group leaders are leading a smaller group of priests! Talk about a seismic shift in thinking. Part of the group leader's role is not to do everything for them, to help them understand their identity in Christ.

From the Group

God has changed my values in terms of what is most important to me. No longer am I fixated on the next purchase, promotion, or potential merit increase. He has opened my heart to be there for other people.

—CHRIS

What Now?

- What is the primary purpose of your groups? Teaching, connecting, serving, or inviting?
- What internal changes do you need to make to empower groups to accomplish that purpose?

5
The Right Leaders

LeaderSpeak

> *Leaders who are deeply impacted by God are able to facilitate holistic, meaningful life change in others. We need both more leaders and better leaders.*
> —Robert E. Logan, *From Followers to Leaders*[1]

Next Step: *Discover and develop the right leaders.*

John and Connie had led groups before. Divorce recovery groups and more traditional classes were entries on their ministry résumé But the challenges changed with an open-ended, year-round group that met in their home.

Classes are often more knowledge based, and other groups normally have clear beginnings and endings (Divorce Care, Celebrate Recovery, Financial Peace). Yet both have tremendous transformation potential. The challenges John and Connie faced in their new group were different from those they faced previously. Now the focus was more balanced between study and relationships. The meeting lasted two hours so there was plenty of time to relate both formally and informally.

John immediately found that the new rules of group life in his home matched his personality and the same for Connie. They were great hosts who made everyone feel welcome. And although it took some time, the group became a family. John said, "Slowly over time the people in the group began to matter to one another."

"The hard part is the energy and time commitments that are needed as you become more involved in each other's lives," John said. "You reach the point where you don't have any more capacity, and that is frustrating, . . . but you can't do it all." Watching people grow in Christ, generosity, and friendship with one another makes it all worth it according to John.

John believes he is the big winner because he is the group leader. The group has been used by God in John's growth.

> God continues to change me. Through the various groups
> I've been part of over the years, I continue to learn to be
> patient with others, seek to understand them, and not
> judge them. As I am doing this, God is using them to show
> me aspects of His Word, which I would not have seen on
> my own. Other people, especially when they are diverse
> from ourselves, help us grow.

John and Connie were the right leaders, but the right leaders are not always easy to find. Leading a group is a tremendous commitment, and leading one in one's own home doubles the commitment. So if you find people willing to make the commitment and who are also good teachers, then normally they're in, with no questions asked. After all, that seems to make the most sense. But other criteria are critically important according to our research.

John and Connie have qualities that are critical in their diverse group, like patience. People need to talk about themselves in their group meetings. Honest disclosure actually causes the group to share life on a deeper level. According to our LifeWay Research survey, 72 percent of people believed that one of the most important characteristics in group leaders is that they make "people feel comfortable sharing in the group."

Leaders in local churches have various gifts and passions. All of them don't need to be your small group leaders. But for your purposes of developing a healthy group life, you need to identify a group leader who is a person of character and who has the leadership DNA that best matches your group strategy. This cannot be stated firmly enough. Matching leadership qualities with the strategy you have selected for your church can make or break your group strategy.

You will need to determine the primary purpose of your groups as it fits into the overall discipleship plan before you choose leaders. As a reminder, the three options for the primary purpose of a group are: (1) formation (teaching and study), (2) connection (connecting believers in biblical community), and (3) mission (serving on mission together).

If you decide that, in your overall discipleship strategy, groups are the environment that bears the primary responsibility for teaching and formation, then you should recruit and develop leaders who will teach people well. You should look for leaders with the gift of teaching, develop them in this gift, and provide training as they teach and lead groups.

If, however, you decide that in your overall discipleship strategy groups will be used primarily for connection and community, then you should recruit and develop leaders who can excel in building community, in relationally shepherding people, in offering hospitality, and in encouraging individuals. You should offer training and development for these leaders to help them shepherd people.

But if you decide that in your church, in light of your established discipleship strategy, groups are predominately about mission engagement, then you should recruit leaders who are evangelistic, who love their local communities and are burdened to lead others in engaging the broader community. You should offer training on learning the cultural nuances of a local community, listening to the needs of the city, and rallying people around a shared mission.

Leadership Matters

That's what the research shows us. To say leadership matters is no shocking revelation, but it is important nonetheless. The bigger questions are: What attributes define group leaders? And which of these attributes are effective in having a successful group?

Group attendees were asked, "Which, if any, of the following describe the leader/facilitator of your small class or group?" Individuals were allowed to select as many attributes as they wanted. The table below shows the results.

Attribute	Percent
Makes people feel comfortable sharing in the group	72%
A good leader	71%
Trustworthy	69%
A good Bible teacher	67%
A good listener	61%
Energetic and enthusiastic	60%
Transparent in his or her own weaknesses and struggles	51%
A personal friend	40%
Skillful in handling conflict or problems in the group	40%
Freely delegates responsibilities within the group	37%
None of these	2%

Nearly two-thirds of respondents selected these attributes: "makes people feel comfortable sharing in the group" (72%), "a good leader" (71%), "trustworthy" (69%), and "a good Bible teacher"

(67%). The only attributes selected by less than half of the respondents are: "a personal friend" (40%), "skillful in handling conflict or problems in the group" (40%), and "freely delegates responsibilities within the group" (37%). A very small percentage of respondents chose "none of these" (2%) for their leader/facilitator.

Nonattenders were similarly asked what attributes they want in a leader/facilitator. The only attribute selected by a majority of respondents was "makes people feel comfortable sharing in a group" (56%). The only other attributes selected by at least 40 percent of the nonattenders were: "a good Bible teacher" (42%) and "trustworthy" (40%). The attribute selected by the least number of nonattenders was "a personal friend" (4%).

From this we see that making people feel comfortable sharing should be an attribute of every small-group leader. It is illuminating that nonattenders are looking for this attribute more than any other. Being a good Bible teacher should not be ignored, but it is not necessarily the most important attribute, at least in the eyes of those engaged in group life, and those who potentially might become involved. Finally, people are not looking for a personal friend to lead/facilitate their small group.

Leader Skills = Ministry Outcomes

For our research we measured outcomes from some basic functions of a group. This simplified what we really were eager to learn and helped us realize that certain skills demonstrated by a group leader influence group outcomes. This may inform not only how a leader is selected but also how leaders are trained, coached, and resourced.

The four outcomes were: serving others, following Christ more closely, evangelism, and growing in community with each other. It is impossible to *fully* explain all of the data, but in our judgment the kind of environment you want to create in your groups can be highly influenced by your leadership. In other words, choosing the right type of leader is among the most important steps you take in shaping the group life in your church.

Several skills were observed among group leaders in our research. The skills of the leaders greatly impacted the culture and the emphasis of the groups the leaders lead. All of these skills are desirable. And while you may want to develop your leaders to take all these skills, knowing the purpose of your groups will help you know which skills are most essential in your leaders.

Remember the relevance of this research. Your mission is to make world-impacting disciples who are transformed and yet still transforming. This is done by creating environments that influence and shape your leaders through relationships, not rules. As a pastor, associate pastor, or groups pastor overseeing small groups, you can either try to control (short-term results) or influence (long-term results).

One way to shape your training, coaching, and resourcing is to focus on the specific leadership attributes that produce ministry outcomes. We encourage you to resist the temptation to take too many. Three or four are more than enough to put a high level of intentionality in what you do to make disciples. Design training around these skills.

1. Leader Skill: Teaching = Ministry Result: Formation and Evangelism
2. Leader Skill: Transparency and Conflict Resolution = Ministry Result: Community and Connection
3. Leader Skill: Delegation = Ministry Result: Mission Engagement

Build formal and informal discussions around your chosen leader attributes. Design coaching templates based on them. Provide articles and books that reinforce them. And have best practices dialogues when groups meet for the monthly or quarterly leadership huddles.

Be creative, but remember, ultimately these attributes need to be embedded in your culture. This is not solely an organic enterprise. As you change the conversations, building them around these, you will change the culture. A culture change serves as a long-term influence on your leaders and group attenders. Examine the following three attributes before determining which kind of leader is needed for your overall disciple-making process.

Teaching: Formation

Groups that grow in their confidence of the Word are often led by leaders who are skilled in teaching. In our research we found that groups that value "evangelism" characterize their leaders as "good Bible teachers." Good Bible teachers help people in groups grow in faith. Paul explained the origin of faith in one of the great evangelistic chapters in the Bible: "So faith comes from what is heard, and what is heard comes through the message about Christ" (Rom. 10:17).

Another significant finding—something we suspected, but that was validated in the research—is this: those who are in groups also shared their faith more and at a much higher rate than those not involved in a group. Basically this is saying that group life impacts how people relate to the unchurched world. It is so much easier for someone who's in a group to articulate his or her faith to someone who's a nonbeliever because in a group setting group members learn how to talk. They get comfortable talking about spiritual things and learn how to share what the Lord is doing in their lives.

From a research vantage point we can say there is a significant relationship between a believer engaged in personal evangelism and a believer engaged in a small group. The people in your church who are plugged into a group are much more likely to be articulating the gospel this week. Why is this? Here are three reasons:

1. *Those in a group learn to discuss spiritual truth.* Those believers in a church who only attend a weekend worship service or large gatherings where they listen to a primary teacher are never in

environments where they speak. They only listen. Thus they don't grow more and more comfortable discussing the faith. Those connected to a small group are in an environment where they share, they verbalize, and they speak about spiritual matters. Thus they are much more comfortable telling the guy in the next cubicle about Jesus and His gracious work.

2. *Those in a group understand growth happens in relationships.* Those who are plugged into a group have likely seen the Lord supernaturally mature people over time in the context of community. They have learned that the Lord uses relationships grounded in grace to transform people. Thus they are likely to see their relationships at work, school, and in their neighborhoods as holy opportunities to invest in people who don't yet know the Lord.

3. *Those in a small group have moved beyond "Sunday only" Christianity.* Those believers plugged into a small group are not merely showing up for a worship service each week. Thus they are more likely to see how their faith impacts the totality of their lives, including regular encounters with unbelievers.

Transparency and Conflict Resolution: Community

Groups that excel in connection, in growing in community with one another, are often led by leaders who excel in transparency and in conflict resolution.

Being real with your group encourages more transparency throughout the group. How do you train, coach, or resource people on how to be transparent about their own weaknesses and struggles? Be transparent about your own struggles with them. Model telling "grace stories" about how God has changed your life in particular.

Someone said once, "Hollywood is great at making fake things look real, but Christians are great at making real things look fake."[2] As a leader, if you never share the darker parts of your life, then you are making Christianity look fake. People assume a lot about leaders—where they are with Christ and how they got there. But most people do not trust the leader who appears to have everything together.

Leaders (pastors in particular) often let their pride cause them to want to live up to what people think of them. Unfortunately the roots of moral failure among Christian leaders can be the moral and spiritual fatigue that builds in by trying to live up to what people expect.

Part of the Transformational Groups project included an open-ended question survey for people actually in groups to see what we could discover. Certain patterns emerged from their responses. Consistently they all feared attending a group, but somehow they got over it enough to get in one. They were afraid of being judged or not fitting into the group. But they had positive experiences once they connected. Here are some sample comments about transparency:

- "I realized Satan wants us to think our struggles and temptation are unique to us."
- "My group helps me not feel alone in my trials."
- "My group gives me a place to share my concerns, questions, and confusion about life."
- "I realize others struggle, even those that seem to have it all together. It's a continual reminder that life's not 'all about me.'"

A group leader who excels in building community among those in the group is also savvy in conflict resolution. All group leaders will need to learn this trait to some degree. "The peacemakers are blessed, for they will be called sons of God" (Matt. 5:9).

Inevitably in groups political and social issues will arise. Opinions about truth and Bible doctrine will emerge. Disagreements and hurt feelings within the group will emerge. And even more awkward are issues concerning the decisions and direction of your church. Why does the church ask for money? Why was a pastoral staff member terminated? Why do church leaders believe we need another new building? The questions are endless. The group leader is the first person many will ask about things like this. The group leader needs to know how to shepherd the hearts of the group without being defensive.

The specific connection between a group leader who is good at handling conflict in the group and the outcome is impossible to directly correlate. However, we suggest that as groups learn to process their differences openly and honestly, unity is established. It is up to the skilled group leader to teach and model biblical conflict resolution. As group leaders do this, the group learns a healthy sense of respect for one another and begins to value their diversity. Then they realize potential to serve others more effectively together than as individuals.

If connection and community are not the primary purpose of your groups, your people will still benefit from leaders who are being trained in transparency and conflict resolution. There is one more leader to examine.

Delegation: Mission

Groups that value serving characterize their leaders as ones who freely delegate responsibilities to the group. The group leader is able to invite others to be involved in serving those the group has accepted responsibility for. This leadership characteristic connects to the unity felt in the group as well as healthy ownership.

Transformation and leadership development should be the obsession of healthy group leaders. Leaders should be trained, coached, and resourced accordingly. Although spiritual babies or unborn babies may be walking in the door, the group leader who wants (or needs) them to remain as such forever has no vision.

Having a new baby is one of life's greatest experiences. As babies grow, they go through phases of development. When a baby rolls over for the first time, it is monumental. Parents take pictures and call grandparents. But as a child progresses from sitting up to crawling and then walking, the excitement continues. And sitting up is not celebrated as much. Although the first day of kindergarten can cause all kinds of emotions, ultimately an emotionally healthy parent celebrates. They prepare for and celebrate growth. They celebrate graduations, weddings, first jobs, and watching their babies become parents.

As he often did, Paul used parental language when addressing the Thessalonians.

> Although we could have been a burden as Christ's apostles, instead we were gentle among you, as a nursing mother nurtures her own children. We cared so much for you that we were pleased to share with you not only the gospel of God but also our own lives, because you had become dear to us. (1 Thess. 2:7–8)

But later Paul described what made the investment worth the effort. He explained:

> For now we live, if you stand firm in the Lord. How can we thank God for you in return for all the joy we experience before our God because of you. (1 Thess. 3:8–9)

Paul took great encouragement in the fact that Christians in Thessalonica were standing up all by themselves for God. He said now we live (*zaō*) or our existence is taken to another level of great, fully alive and most excited because of the maturity of his spiritual family. Paul was enjoying another phase of life in his children—full spiritual adulthood—and much of it worked out in his absence. This is often the result of delegation.

Delegation is consistent with the ministry target of Ephesians 4—equipping for those who have been called to lead and develop. Don't be timid about asking people to take on responsibility. Your goal should always be to push them faster than they feel ready to go. Just like teaching your child to ride a bike. They may not feel like they can do it without training wheels. They may beg you not to let go of the bike. But eventually, after hopefully not too many falls, they learn to do it on their own, and they take off and go with the training you have given them.

If you continually hang on to the bike or you treat your group leaders like customers, they will remain customers—good luck with that. They will never grow, and you will not have enough hours in the day or hands to hold all the group leaders wobbling along on their bikes, afraid to do it on their own. To treat them like owners will help them own.

And when they stand up on their own, throw them a bigger party than they deserve! Celebrate like you should when a child learns to ride a bike. It will be really fun, and you will plant seeds in those who are still customers.

Discovering and Developing Leaders

While many church leaders understand the merit and need for small groups in our culture, the actual implementation of the small groups can seem somewhat daunting. Leader discovery and development is especially critical. Here are some preliminary discovery steps.

Define the leader's role and responsibilities. The best people you ask to consider God's call to lead a group will need information. They need ample opportunity to pray, kick the tires, and ask questions about group leadership. You want that too. In the human resources world they often say, "There are no such thing as firing, just bad hiring." The same could be said about the group. You will save yourself a lot of headaches and move the mission of God farther faster if you are extremely intentional on the front end. From consideration to small-group leadership deployment and beyond, there should be a clear path the leadership team clearly explains. That builds a healthy group culture.

One of the first questions each pastor needs to ask is, "How much of the function of regular church life do you want to push to the edge of church life?" Go as far as you can to allow the group to take on the life of the church—to be a church *of* small groups and not a church *with* small groups. That is a significant and substantial difference.

There will be limits to that (unless you want to be a house church and no longer have the public gathering). However, think through what you can do. For example, can small groups practice the ordinance of the Lord's Supper together during their regular meeting time? Do you want to call them "lay pastors"? Etc.

Regardless, most people seem to agree that small groups should be empowered to win people to Christ, serve others, and hold one another accountable. As such, certain criteria should be in place for someone to lead these responsibilities.

Remove barriers to leadership by using carefully chosen terminology. Oftentimes capable group leaders are hesitant to become leaders because they believe they are incapable of accomplishing what is necessary. And in many instances this is due to the terminology a church uses to describe the person who leads the group. For instance, in some blue-collar cultures the term *leader* conjures up the idea that the person spearheading the group is like the manager at the plant or the boss man at work. Not only will there be a cringe factor when the term is used; it also leads working-class people to believe they are not smart enough or leader enough to take on the role of shepherding a group. In these settings the term *host* would be a much better option than *leader* when describing the person spearheading a group.

Find people who are passionate about people and groups. While it may seem antithetical, many times these people are those who challenge your leadership in an appropriate, biblical fashion. Think about it. Probably one of the reasons you became a leader is that you felt a call to do something you saw others do. In many cases a small group leader may feel that same passion on a smaller scale.

Isn't that what you want? People who feel a strong calling to be a part of one of your most important transformational platforms are your friends and friends of God's mission. They want to learn more about sermons and want others to do so as well. Look for people who want to talk more about your sermons, and give them a platform to lead others in a group setting.

Other small-group leader qualities are difficult to teach. Are they gifted leaders you can personally connect with and who can affirm others? Do they have a spirit of servanthood? Are they regularly encouraging others? Are they coachable?

Assess their natural, spiritual, and social qualifications. They need to exhibit natural spiritual, emotional, and social qualifications. It's possible to love Jesus and be kind of creepy. I have a great pastor friend who is a phenomenal teacher but wouldn't be the best small-group leader. It's not that he has poor hygiene; he just has a tendency to blurt things out and be somewhat socially awkward in smaller situations. Small-group leaders need naturally to create a community of learning together.

Lastly, you need to actively pray for these leaders and be on the lookout for God to point them out. A natural "testing ground" for potential leaders is to have them first serve as an "apprentice leader" under a more established leader. Whenever Ed starts a new group at Grace Church, they ask each group leader to also select an apprentice they will train, encourage, and pastor to take a group of their own. Regular prayer through this process is vital to successful leader implementation.

Leading a groups' disciple-making process requires careful thought, prayer, and planning. The primary role is an equipper.

Become an Equipper

The loneliest person in a local church is not the single mother in her thirties with her three preschool children. Neither is it the widower who recently lost his wife after being married over fifty years. The loneliest person in the local church is often the one standing beside a clipboard in the lobby waiting for people to sign up to serve. We believe it is the most dangerous and nonproductive approach for discovering and deploying servant leaders.

Desperation drives us to the lobby-clipboard method of enlist-ment. *No matter the number needed or the size of your vision, finding enough of the right leaders is everything.* You may want to back up and read that sentence again . . . here, we'll help you. *No matter the number needed or the size of your vision, finding enough of the right leaders is everything.*

Ephesians 4 addressed this incredible need for people to do local church ministry. The principles are timeless, practical, and the kind of ministry God empowers. But it also becomes a litmus test of how to do "the work of the ministry" well. God has given "people gifts" to the local church that all have specific motivating factors and passions (apostle, prophet, evangelist, pastor-teacher). We addressed this in chapter 3.

As the local church pursues the mission of God in the world, their God-given leadership provides balance so the church does not become all about one thing. This Spirit-empowered ministry model leverages the gospel effectiveness of any church, any size, in any location.

Churches have unique footprints based on context and makeup, but ultimately all churches are to pursue the same biblical mission. So all churches are the same, and all churches are different . . . like people. In what ways are churches the same?

One way all churches are the same is that they need a constant flow of God-called and motivated, volunteer ministers. Paid pastoral ministry professionals are normally an asset to the mission depend-ing on their Ephesians 4 motivating factors and passions. But their view of their purpose on the team is critical. Ministry responsibili-ties they help staff range from helping the poor in the community to helping park cars on Sunday and, of course, leading groups.

Now the purpose of the Ephesians 4 gifting is "for the training of the saints in the work of ministry, to build up the body of Christ" (Eph. 4:12). The investment of God-called pastors and volunteer ministry directors is about discovering, developing, and deploying volunteer ministers. We hold that Scripture is God breathed and truth without any mixture of error, but at times all of us have been guilty of loving the ministry more than the ministers. God is telling us exactly how to do something important here. But in practice we read Ephesians 4:11–12 another way:

> And He personally gave some to be apostles, some prophets, some evangelists, some pastors and teachers, for ~~the training of the saints in~~ the work of ministry, to build up the body of Christ. (deletion ours)

As pastors and leaders, we aspire to do God's work, God's way. But too often our actual behavior is to do God's work, our way—meaning, we do it ourselves as opposed to helping others do it. If we can see our ministry is to empower others to do ministry, it changes our approach almost entirely.

Ephesians 4 reveals the diverse gifting of the local church for doing ministry, and building the body builds supernatural unity. God-energized unity is the best and only kind, particularly for His local church. Making unity happen in the flesh is messy and ineffective.

Churches are in chaos because of their lack of practical application of these truths. Infighting and mistrust are based on our blindness to our diversity. And the devastating eternal effect is the hindrance of the gospel in our communities. Men, women, and children are without the gospel witness God had planned for them to receive from us because we simply cannot get along.

How can diverse gifting actually build unity in the body of Christ? Because we all need one another to be effective in the mission. We cannot survive by ourselves and be effective for God because we don't have all the gifting necessary. So we need you no matter if we are passionate about the same things or motivated the same way. We need one another even if we don't particularly like one another. If our passion is the mission, then no believer can be left behind! The whole body is needed and is uniquely arranged for the good of all. Paul concluded:

From Him the whole body, fitted and knit together by
every supporting ligament, promotes the growth of the
body for building up itself in love by the proper working of
each individual part. (Eph. 4:16)

The E-Myth Revisited, written by Michael Gerber, is one of the
most popular business books ever written. Gerber's main point is
that most businesses are started by technicians or what we might
call practitioners.[3] That is why most businesses fail. Why is this true?

Gerber tells a story about a woman who was so incredible at
making apple pies that she decided, with the encouragement of her
friends, to start a business. But the business was failing, and she was
on the verge of collapse. What she really loved to do was make apple
pies, and people loved them. But she had no managerial or entrepre-
neurial skills so her business was doomed to fail.

All of us began as ministry practitioners or technicians in one
way or another just like the apple pie lady. We were not born to
reproduce leaders or systems on a high level. The answer is to function with joy within your most useful place and work to develop
other skills to be ready to take another role if needed.

Regardless of when we met Christ, we soon began to serve
God and love it. As time evolved and our skills developed, people
began to notice and invite us to do more. But the tension was, at
least initially, that we had to leave an age group we loved being with
(children, youth, senior adults) or a marginalized group (the poor,
widow, orphans) in order to "do more."

Now you have been asked to be the volunteer youth director.
You can afford to think like the apple pie lady from Gerber's book. If
you do well, it will mean less time with youth, more time with parents and youth leaders. This is the important moment of clarity as
God gives volunteers, paid staff, or pastors greater responsibility. Are
you willing to surrender your love for hands-on ministry and trans-
fer that to love for ministers? If God is calling you to do more, this is
what He is asking you to do. And there is no shame to saying no at

this point. God doesn't call or need everybody to lead and develop leaders. God needs those who will serve in other ways too.

Are we suggesting that ministry should no longer be important to you? No. In fact, we are suggesting that ministry should become more important to you because you want more people to be touched by God through ministry. And you understand that the gospel needs to go farther than you can ever take it all yourself. You love Jesus and the gospel so much you want more people to be influenced. So, in order to do that, you must reproduce yourselves in others and have them reproduce themselves in others too.

Pastoral staff and volunteer ministry directors in healthy, biblical churches fully embrace the importance of leadership development to the future influence for the kingdom. Look for positional ministry leaders who get this on a high level. Volunteer and leader discovery is NOT a necessary evil in an otherwise great chance to do ministry. Volunteer and leader discovery IS ministry. Some of you may already be gifted for this, but you have resisted because you saw this as a division in ministry effectiveness rather than a multiplication of ministry. Whom can you equip for greater disciple making?

Erroneous Defaults

If you are ready to embrace God's assignment and gifting as an equipper, then you have to begin the process of finding people to equip. Finding the right people is highly relational, labor intensive, and deeply intentional. But understanding and embracing your role is an important first step. Now you know the vast majority of your time should and will go into this process.

However, when you combine the incredible need for effective group leaders with the limited supply, you could easily default to some common and erroneous ways of finding them. We have made these mistakes, and that's why we are so good at explaining them.

Be careful of five types of people to use as group leaders:

1. The person who is ready. If you deploy a teaching veteran who just joined your church from First Harmony United Church, you will end up doing groups the way they did them at First Harmony. The veteran from First Harmony has a high God IQ but may unfortunately come with all types of agendas and opinions about how to do groups. You want to replicate the DNA of *your church's* strategy, not someone else's. They may have something you can employ in your groups that can help the overall structure so don't dismiss them entirely.

So we are not saying to avoid the mature believer but to recognize that it will take time to rewire their instincts as a group leader. You need everyone on the same page for good disciple making to take place in groups.

2. The person who is willing. There's a place for willing people in your church. Don't set them up for failure and give a bad experience for people who are searching for community. No matter where servant leaders are deployed, they do have to be . . . willing, right? But the point here is that if *willing* is their only motivating factor, then group leading is not their sweet spot.

If we are not careful, we can take willing people, hand them the latest study, and boom! We have community, or we tell ourselves we do. So, yes, this may look like a short-term solution, but you are looking for long-term solutions and viral disciple making. Being willing is just not enough to make a great group leader.

3. The person who is able. A couple with a big house and plenty of discretionary cash to buy great refreshments each week is tempting, we confess. If they have both of those characteristics, they are probably successful at something, too. What a perfect world! Plenty of really nice space and none of the group members need to stop at the store on the way to the meeting! They may have everything you could want—right demographic, right job, nice house, people like them—but do they have a single focus? Are they willing to take spiritual responsibility for a group of people?

4. The person with a résumé. The former pastor who is between churches and the missionary on furlough are wonderful to have around if they'll share in your vision. Seminary students, denominational leaders, or former nonprofit ministry leaders can bring excellent skills to your body and your small groups. Yet don't assume they are your next great group leaders. They normally walk in the door with a passion to serve and a willingness to do whatever you ask. But how long will they be at your church? How many weekends will they be committed elsewhere?

The question isn't if you will use the person with a résumé. The question is, how can you maximize their gifts, experience, and perspectives while you have them? For example, if you have fifteen to twenty group leaders, how many of them could use a mentor/coach? This may be a great way to multiply their gifts without placing them over a single group.

Remember, your commitment to create transformational environments is a commitment to influence, not control. The primary way you control is through rules, standards, and the clear enforcement of such. The primary way you influence is through consistent, caring relational environments. So, after getting to know this veteran leader God has sent you, assign them to mentor/coach a cluster of group leaders. Encourage them to do lunch and life with those leaders if for no other reason than to encourage and bless them. You then have leveraged this leader for the vision God has given you for life change.

5. The person who is reluctant. Leaders from the Bible like Moses, David, and Jeremiah were known for their hesitancy to lead when God asked. But at times we confuse humility with real reluctance. The profile of this leader is the opposite of the veteran teacher who wants to lead a group ASAP in order to exercise their teaching gift. We figure something has to be right about one who is so humble they say no to your first ask.

Humility is one thing—maybe someone feels overwhelmed by the request and has a really high view of the position. Again, that is a good thing. But reluctance or an unwillingness to lead could be for multiple reasons, some very personal. For example, the person could have a secret sin problem—a habit or addiction that they can't really surrender or talk about. Maybe marriage or family issues are causing pressure. Continue the conversation, and don't be afraid to ask tougher questions. This may be God's way of rescuing the person. But drop the group leader thoughts if you are getting serious resistance.

If groups are essential in your disciple-making strategy, resist the urge to succumb to these defaults. Discover and develop leaders with great intentionality.

From the Group

God has shown me that even though I may not be the most knowledgeable person when it comes to the Bible, I can still help lead a men's group. God has helped me grow closer to Him by convicting me to step out of my comfort zone.

—CHRIS

What Now?

- Design a path of group leadership discovery and development that starts with the first conversation and goes through the leader's first full year of group leadership.

6
Group Practices

LeaderSpeak

If we can connect to God and to one another, we can
pretty much shape the world together.
—Joey Bonifacio, *The LEGO Principle*[1]

Next Step: *Define your group practices.*

Saundra was a young single mother who had made some tough, life-affecting decisions. Yet she was perfectly willing to give God at least one more try. So she went back to her parents' church and looked for a group to make connections. She was not married at the time and expecting her third child.

The group to which she was invited was not what you would have normally prescribed for an expectant single mom in her late twenties. Her life situation matched no one else's in the group. She was the youngest in the group. The group had some older single adults: one widow, two divorcees, and some married but attending alone. The youngest person in the group other than Saundra was a married woman attending alone.

Saundra enjoyed the style of church, but her only hope for transformation was to connect to life-giving relationships. Younger, more contemporary churches were within driving distance, but contemporary style provided no long-term solution for her spiritual needs. Her only hope was community. She had burned some bridges so there were places she could no longer go for support. But these new bridges into the lives of passionate, loving, nonjudgmental believers had yet to be crossed.

Saundra explained more of her backstory:

> I used to live a very rough life working in bars, drinking, and not spending enough time with the people that really mattered. I thought I had tons of friends and was actually crazy enough to be comfortable in that life. I was keeping myself constantly distracted from the reality of what I needed.

Her journey back to God included taking the bold step of trying a group. "I was hesitant to join a small group for fear that I wouldn't belong." Saundra said, "I thought the people wouldn't genuinely care about me because of all of the 'friends' from my past life."

But she was surprised by the incredible connection she made with a group of people who accepted and loved her. She experienced their unconditional love through babysitting and baby showers as well as help with building a résumé and searching for a job. She built deep Christian friendships like she had never experienced before. She crossed bridges that she could not possibly afford to burn. And God changed everything for her.

Saundra gave a picture of life before and then life after her turnaround, "I had always fought with fears of inadequacy prior to having these amazing examples of Christians around me who are transparent enough to show that they are human too." She knew God used her group for her transformation:

Without the support of a group, I wouldn't have been reading the Bible daily or have become involved in inner-city ministry to love all of the wonderful people there. I am very grateful. . . . I am honestly not sure where my life would be right now without my friends from my small group.

Saundra's story illustrates a key finding in LifeWay Research's findings. Her involvement in groups directly influenced an increase in her use of spiritual disciplines and engagement in ministry. But the transformational influence goes beyond outward behaviors. Evidence of a seismic shift in values was discovered through observing her life over an extended period of time as well as through her interview. The group was the vehicle through which the Holy Spirit delivered transformation.

Modern Research

Modern research studies often discover principles that Christians know to be true—truths about life and humanity already disclosed by God in Scripture. This should not be surprising to us because whether the researcher is a believer or not, research studies typically examine an aspect of God's general revelation—humanity.

For example, one of the most seminal leadership books in the last fifty years was *Servant Leadership* by Robert Greenleaf. Long before Greenleaf's paradigm-altering book, Jesus demonstrated and encouraged leadership through service. In the same way many studies show the adverse affects divorce has on children. And long before those studies made their way into academic journals, the Lord declared His hatred of divorce.

Harvard on Groups

Todd Heatherton and Patricia Nichols led a Harvard study to examine factors that contributed to people radically changing their lives. They wondered, "What causes someone to become completely different in his approach to life, his habits, his relationships, and his priorities?" The two factors they found for contributing to change were interesting.[2]

First, they discovered that tragedy often leads to change. The tragedy may be personal, or it may be observed in someone else. The Scripture, of course, teaches that the Lord will use personal trials and struggles to mature us and form us more into the image of His Son.

Second, the researchers discovered that in some cases no tragedy is involved in change. Rather, community is. Community serves as the catalyst for change. One of the researchers, Todd Heatherton, commented, "Change occurs among other people." This is no surprise for followers of Jesus and students of Scripture. The Lord has supernaturally ordained Christian community to mature His people.

Other people rubbing against us, challenging us, and encouraging us has a sanctifying effect on our lives. The writer of the book of Hebrews challenges us to "encourage each other daily, while it is still called today, so that none of you is hardened by sin's deception" (Heb. 3:13). Encouragement from a community of Christ followers keeps us soft before the Lord. Without community we are likely to grow cold in our walk with the Lord.

Far more important than changing habits, priorities, or behavior is the transformation of the heart. Only Jesus has the power to transform us, and He uses others to nudge us along in our relationship with Him. Community that is Christian, community that is grounded in the grace of God, is essential for the ongoing transformation of the heart.

While groups grounded in Jesus and the Word are deeply transformational, our research indicates that far too many churches saddle their groups with too many expectations. We discovered that the most impactful groups were the ones with the most clarity about their focus and with the ones with leaders appropriately matched to their groups. Sadly, we also discovered that clarity is often lacking. Many pastors ask their groups to do everything, thus they do not excel at much of anything.

Top Five Activities Pastors Expect in Their Groups

Out of one thousand phone interviews with pastors:

1. Bible Study   97%
2. Prayer   95%
3. Care   85%
4. Inviting Others   79%
5. Socializing   78%

Keep in mind that out of the thousand pastors surveyed, we can conclude each has high and sometimes unrealistic expectations concerning small-group deliverables. The bottom three of the list of eight activities the pastors could have chosen were:

6. Connect Socially between Meetings   68%
7. Serve People outside the Church   65%
8. Follow Up with Church Visitors   60%

When you add another seismic stat—83 percent of a thousand pastors expected five or more of these activities to take place in their small groups—you see a picture of expected deliverables! We would hate to be in charge of "group sales" at those churches—all 83 percent of them! Pastoral expectations appear to have climbed beyond what any church's groups ministry can deliver.

Be Clear about Expectations

As you set out to build what you believe God has helped you design, you are now faced with realistic expectations. The same is true when you are looking to build or buy a new home.

Who wouldn't want a thousand-square foot laundry room that includes plenty of countertop space to sort and fold as well as bars to hang clothes? This would allow your entire family to work comfortably as a team every day in order to stay on top of the laundry.

You can include a huge workout room, located just outside your amazing man cave, complete with dumbbells and your three favorite cardio machines. And don't forget the enormous master suite with two closets the size of bedrooms and a large heart-shaped Jacuzzi bathtub.

You may prefer all of those things, but unless your budget and income stream are dramatically different from average, it's not going to happen.

When you analyze pastoral expectations of group activities from our research, too often we begin to see images of large heart-shaped Jacuzzi bathtubs. If expectations stay at this place, frustration and lethargy are bound to be your destination. Yet focusing those expectations as well as resourcing and coaching toward streamlined, strategic expectations can lead to transformational group outcomes.

Instead of looking at the group process like a new home that can have everything, look at them like designing a computer or smart phone. Trade-offs are expected. You can have the fastest and most powerful computer, but you can't have it *and* the most portable. Your smart phone can have the largest screen, but it can't *also* fit in your pocket. You have to choose the elements that are most valuable to you and compromise on the others.

When thinking about small groups, clarity of values is essential. Marcus Buckingham, *New York Times* best-selling author, motivational speaker, business consultant, and researcher, said, "Clarity is the preoccupation of the effective leader. If you do nothing else as a leader, be clear." Wise church leaders clarify, guard, and preach the essentials over and over again. Pastors must also be continually clear on the ministry philosophy and direction of the church and of small groups. People long to have a direction painted for them, to see how all the church does is built on the theology and philosophy of ministry that drives the church. Pastors who fail to offer directional clarity leave a massive vacuum of leadership. Consequently, others will step in with competing visions of what the church should be and do. And the church will move in a plethora of directions, unsure of who she really is.

This is especially true in group life. Because so many churches give so much freedom to their group leaders, the ideological vacuum is immense. On many occasions while consulting a church about groups, the groups pastor mentions the inability to get done what needs to be accomplished. Some of the groups just get together and have a weekly pity party, others are all about fun and games, and others just get together to have dinner and discuss whatever is on someone's mind. When asked what the groups were told to do and what they are to focus on, in almost every instance the response goes something like this, "I told them that they needed to get together and do life together." Leaders need clarity, and if the church leadership doesn't clarify precisely what needs to happen and equip the leader to do that, the group leader will do whatever seems most natural and demands the least of them.

Where do you start? How can you bring clarity to your group practices, to what your groups value, and to how they function? That is for you to determine in your context. How many behaviors are possible for one group? See the previous answer. But here are some tips to help create this important list.

1. Discuss the options with the church staff, particularly your pastor, about expectations.
2. Empower key group leaders by involving them in the discussion. This builds ownership that will influence groups and other group leaders.
3. Examine your context for clues. Search for unique needs and strengths from other ministries of your church that do not need duplicating.

4. Integrate outcomes with the overall disciple-making strategy of your church.
5. Pray and invite others into a season of prayer. Trust God to build what He wants through your groups.

Remember, certain behaviors tend to produce certain outcomes. Make your choices and then train, coach, and resource accordingly. We compiled this list with the help of an informal poll of pastors, church planters, group pastors, and group leaders. Consider the following group practices a menu of options:

Practice Spiritual Disciplines Together (Prayer, Bible Study, Worship)

Regardless of where your group meets, practicing spiritual disciplines has great impact. Even in a relational group this helps move the focus Godward. Practicing the disciplines together becomes an advertisement (and teaching moment) for people to practice them when they are alone. For those who are new to faith, the disciplines are a "show how" moment for them, too.

The group can consider other disciplines. As mentioned before, some groups may be free to serve the Lord's Supper in their homes. They can emphasize seasons of prayer, fasting, solitude, and journaling. Certain group studies may include the discipline of journaling to run concurrent with the study.

One group was going through a study on prayer. They decided to practice prayer with more intentionality rather than just study it. The meetings included extended times of prayer. They each practiced journaling during the time and shared some of their discoveries with the group. Finally, they fasted as a group—some for the first time ever. They ended their group fast with a shared meal at their next group meeting.

Care for One Another During Life's Evolutions (Birth, Death, Marriage, Graduation, etc.)

Nothing says doing life together more than weddings and funerals. Traditionally, the pastoral staff is the primary delivery system for ministry during life events, but groups taking a high level ownership of life evolutions are more caring and Christlike. Not only is the care more personal, but also groups have more bandwidth to do ministry than a pastoral staff.

Paul described Christians in community with family-related terms. He described life together in Romans 12—this would make a great chapter for your groups to study. Laughing and crying together are ways we become family. Paul said, "Rejoice with those who rejoice; weep with those who weep" (Rom. 12:15). If pastors and staff would step back and let groups care more, they would help groups grow deeper in community. Pastors hurt group development when they insist on being the alpha in crisis situations.

Schedule Time with One Another between Regular Meetings

One way to measure the health of your groups is in their relational connections between meetings. Regardless of your feelings about the pros and the cons of the technology revolution, the ability to stay connected has never been easier. Texting, Facebooking, Twittering, and blogging is the language of a generation and generations to come. Some churches implement an in-house technological communication for members to talk to one another. The City, Cobblestone Network, and Church Community Builder are some tools out there for the church. Groups can use these forums to communicate with one another and share prayer needs privately.

Some of the deepest discussions and questions about life with God come in those meetings between the meetings. We see this modeled by Jesus with His disciples. Informal conversations are disarming and moments of transparency more frequent. As you measure the effectiveness of your groups, you should ask, "How often are you connecting during the week beyond your regularly scheduled group meetings?"

Have Fun Together

Following Christ where we live, work, and play has become cliché in contemporary churches. But if the subject is "life together," then fun together is part of life. So whether it is in ball games, movies, camping trips, or crowd breakers, the desire to have fun is something we all hold in common. You could even plan to make one of the group meeting nights devoted exclusively to some fun activity.

Serve to Share the Gospel in Word and Deed

Like spiritual disciplines, serving to share the gospel lets groups do together what we hope they will grow to do more on their own. Every serving opportunity may not present itself to sharing the gospel in word. But prayer, preparation, and debriefing should be highly influenced by the motivation that those you serve may see and know Jesus Christ.

Brad House, author of *Community: Taking Your Small Group Off Life Support,* suggests "neighborhood approach" by having groups focus all their efforts on reaching people for Christ in the geographical areas where they meet. Brad explained, "The goal of the neighborhood can be summed up by the idea of saturating the city with the gospel of Jesus Christ. Community groups have the ability to fill every nook and cranny of our city as outposts of the gospel."[3]

Eat Together

References to food, eating, and meals are found throughout the New Testament. In the first description of the early church in Acts 2:42–47, the disciplines listed included eating (breaking bread) twice. Eating together was listed in a pretty elite list of disciplines that include prayer, teaching, giving, and gathering in the temple. Tim Chester, author of *Meals with Jesus: Discovering Grace, Community and Mission around the Table,* summed it up by saying,

"Food connects."[4] We don't all like sports or art or extreme biking, but we have never met a person who didn't eat. Paul knew this to be true:

> Therefore, whether you eat or drink, or whatever you do, do everything for God's glory. (1 Cor. 10:31)

Jesus expressed His heart's desire for a relationship with the lukewarm Laodicean church: "If anyone hears My voice and opens the door, I will come in to him and have dinner with him, and he with Me" (Rev. 3:20). For a church that was not doing well spiritually, an invitation to meet and dine with Jesus must have been a surprise. Jesus surprised the tax collectors and sinners in the same way. Sharing meals is sharing life.

Depending on where and when your group meets, eating during the weekly meeting may not be practical. The between-meetings social gatherings can make up the difference. You can even dedicate one of the group meeting times as a special occasion when you eat a meal together. Eating is so much a part of our lives that sharing life seems deeper when we eat together. Powerful, informal, open conversations often take place at the table.

Open Fellowship Times to Unchurched Friends

Most groups are considered open groups. But as groups begin to "do life" over a longer period of time, assimilating new people is easier said than done. A great bridge for introducing new people to Christ is a party or cookout. Some groups will merge these activities with those evolutionary times in life. Some groups will host baby or wedding showers for friends and family of people in their group. Other groups will have block parties in the neighborhoods where they meet.

Meet Weekly

We know it sounds funny, but we have seen it happen. What if you had a group that seldom met? The practice of meeting weekly is a challenge for some groups, particularly young couples with children. But when you take away summers, holidays, sickness, and vacations as prime meeting times, your window to meet gets small. A meeting rhythm is critical for transformation. Relationships and significant progress in group spiritual disciplines are affected when groups don't meet. Meeting every other week is actually harder than meeting weekly because every week your weekly schedule alters. "Are we meeting THIS week?"

Constant cancellation of meetings leads to frustration in the group. Groups must work hard to establish defaults. Clear hard stops and starts can help for groups, even if they meet in homes. Groups must not be confined to meeting in one location. Obvious cancellations due to holidays, summer, etc., must be planned well in advance. If people in your groups are asking the question: "Are we meeting this week?" leaders need to change the meeting culture of their group.

Metrics/Celebrations/Scorecards

Winston Churchill is known, perhaps more than any other statesman, not only for his brilliant leadership but also for his memorable quotes. While it may not be his most humorous he is credited with, this quote is certainly one worth noting: "However beautiful the strategy, you should occasionally look at the results."[5]

Although outcomes are not 100 percent predictable, no matter your group system, you can expect certain behaviors will influence your preferred outcomes. In chapter 5 you saw a correlation between Bible study and evangelism as well as between delegation and service. Some of the correlations are self-evident. Others may be discovered through paying attention. But in your context you may connect behaviors to outcomes that are unique.

Behaviors, for the most part, are measurable and can be influenced. For example, if you want each group to have their own mission project in your city or community, you can measure that. You can also influence that—not through legislation but through celebration. How do you influence through celebration?

For example, if your groups are new to the idea of serving through their own mission project, you can invite the director of your local homeless shelter to speak to your next leaders' huddle. You can celebrate the importance of the shelter in the city and let group leaders know how they can begin serving there.

Another way to celebrate is to put a spotlight on the first group that begins serving in your community. Let them tell their story in writing, with pictures, and through e-mail. Give them airtime at your next leaders' meeting. And in a best-case scenario, get them Sunday morning time for a sixty-second video commercial. You not only encourage groups and their leaders; you also influence the 80 percent of people who would come to a group if invited.

Our research reveals that people grow most when they are also serving others. So a good scorecard category would measure groups serving. There are lots of ways to do this. For example, ask your small groups to take one night a month to participate in a community-service project, then have them share regular reports on these projects from the leaders telling what they did, who came, and any significant, firsthand stories that may have happened.

In addition, we can have people self-report their service, and other discipleship categories, on an annual spiritual formation instrument. (We use the Transformational Discipleship Assessment (TDA); see www.lifeway.com/tda.) This is a more quantitative measurement of people's health and growth than the qualitative small-group reports. The TDA measures six or seven categories including small-group involvement, service, and personal discipleship.

Clearly these tools are not the end-all for assessing the health and growth of your church. They are a starting point, however. They provide a concrete report that we, as a church, as well as our individual congregational members, can use each year to continually compare our progress and highlight areas of needed focus. It's our way to "promote love and good works" and encourage one another along our journeys.

What you value you measure, and when you measure, you should celebrate. Churches and their groups need a scorecard. It may start with numerical tracking, but it goes beyond that. We need to see not only what we're doing but how well we are doing it. We're doing lots of things to reach people, but are we reaching people? We've got lots of programs to disciple people, but are people really being discipled?

Although we need a scorecard, we don't think the scorecard is everything. We are well aware that there can be a biblically faithful church that is doing everything God tells them to do, and yet it still shrinks in attendance. It can happen, but it's not our desire. A scorecard can help make this more the exception than the rule.

Most scorecards start with purely numerical statistics, often in two main categories: butts and baptisms. How many people are attending each week, making a decision for Christ, and choosing to be baptized? How many groups do you have, and how many are attending these groups? How many new people are attending groups this quarter?

These are obviously important metrics, but we think we should count more. If we count what matters, these things matter, but they're not the only things that matter. Once people make a decision for Christ, are they living changed lives and sharing Christ with their friends and neighbors? If not, I don't think we've ultimately completed the task.

We count people because people count. We track actions and activities because certain practices have proven to result in transformation. Our heart for our community and passion for Jesus drives us to give our lives to ministry and to pursue it to the best of our ability. Taking breaks along the way to see how we're doing is just another way to pursue this calling with excellence.

From the Group

I have met some of the greatest "lead by example men" through small groups. Actually seeing another man live the Christian life is an encouragement. I have drawn closer to God from the presence of these men in my life.

—CLIFF

What Now?

- What are the primary behaviors you want your groups to practice?
- What adjustments need to be made to training, coaching, and resourcing your leaders to enhance these behaviors?

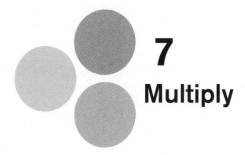

7
Multiply

> *Jesus' circle grew to do even greater things than He did because they were with Him for three years. They watched Him do well at the things they were terrible at.*
> —Artie Davis, *Craveable*[1]

Next Step: *Focus on multiplying groups and disciples.*

Stan Bray was just another church planter with small groups. He had three groups including a new member's class in his new church in Pelzer, South Carolina. These groups met at the church's rented facility in a shopping strip. But then the surprise came, and with the surprise new thinking came about what makes groups work for Real Life Church (www.reallifechurch.cc).

"Most of our people felt that their homes were not nice enough to host a group," Stan said. "But when we began our groups campaign and integrated preaching and age-graded ministries with it, it didn't seem to matter."

Real Life Church prepared people to start new groups in the neighborhoods. They provided invitations to distribute to neighbors and friends. People owned the vision in a big way. Leaders and groups were multiplied as was the gospel influence in the community. Seven new group leaders started groups, and six new host homes were opened.

The number of groups has grown from three groups to eleven. Now more than one hundred people attend small groups. Thirty of those people did not attend Real Life previously. One young lady came to Stan about leading a small group in her home. She had two teenage daughters that came to church with her, but her husband hardly came. She had ten people attend her group, including her husband who seldom attended church. Eight in the group were not Real Life attendees.

Groups meet in the church facility, a local sandwich shop, another restaurant, and in homes. The fact that Stan preaches the material that most groups will use during the week made more people willing to lead. Our research revealed that only 17 percent of the churches surveyed had all classes use the same material. In the case of Real Life, at least, a unified study emphasis helped multiply new groups.

The long-term influence of this surge is yet to be seen, but this is a big step in a new direction. But the possibility for more lives transformed by the gospel has been significantly increased. Real Life Church and pastor Stan Bray also see the incredible potential of groups to go viral in a small community. People really are interested in groups if the time, place, and dynamic are right. Unchurched people are connecting. New people are leading and new groups are forming. And the number of Real Life attenders involved in groups has doubled.

You may have experienced building your own home. Although mental-health professionals consider it a major life stressor, it can also be a dream come true. During the design phase you are making all the right choices, and so is your spouse. You are actually agreeing at times over the size of the office and the master bedroom. The tile and carpet choices were almost without controversy. Then you go into the building phase. Although the pace is slower than you would like, and the materials always seem to arrive late, your dream is starting to take shape.

After this exciting but highly emotional and stressful process is complete, would you possibly consider not moving in and enjoying your new home? Would you be reluctant to use all the space or invite company to enjoy your spacious back deck? Would you still insist on working at the local coffee shop instead of your awesome new office? Absolutely not! You would maximize your investment.

We have just walked through a similar process. You have walked through the design phase of Transformational Group life. You have looked at God's part of taking any method and making it transformational. The biblical base for community, transformation, and groups has been established. You have recognized the need for a discipleship process including the definition of a disciple. You have also learned the importance of integrating groups into your overall church disciple-making strategy.

The building phase included the obvious steps: defining the purpose and values of your groups in light of your overall discipleship strategy, finding the right leader, and defining group behaviors. Like your new house, it is time to move in and maximize what God has given you for His mission. That will include multiplying disciples and groups, as well as imagining the possibilities of a movement.

Five Significant Conclusions

If we review the research from Transformational Groups, we have come to five significant conclusions about groups. Like Real Life Church, it is important that after groups are designed and built they are maximized. As you think about maximizing groups, remember these conclusions:

1. Groups Are Important

Pastors (97% agree) have told us that small groups are an important part of their church. They expect their leadership to be personally involved (97% agree) and use these groups to mobilize their church (76% agree).

2. Groups Are Beneficial

Individuals who regularly attend small groups are consistently making more progress in their spiritual development than those who are not. This is especially true in building relationships within their church. They are more likely to take on responsibilities within their church (63%) including leadership functions. They read (67% at least a few times a week) and study (42% at least a few times a week) the Bible more and have a more consistent prayer life.

They are more actively inviting others to church and sharing their faith. Real Life Church's Sunday morning worship attendance increased 20 percent within the first six weeks of their surge in small groups.

3. Groups Are Needed

A lot of people were no longer attending groups because the group they were in ended and there were no alternatives (32%). People are busy with many activities in their lives, but 80 percent of nonattenders are open to attending groups. The more options available to them through different times, locations, or subjects, the more likely they are to find a viable option for the current nonattenders.

4. Groups Are Variable

The data did not show any magical formula for how groups must be formed. Groups can be of different sizes, meet in different locations, and use different materials. Groups can meet at different times, be established for different reasons, and have leaders with different characteristics. Groups can take on many shapes and sizes and still be effective. Groups do need to consider what their goals are and then incorporate that knowledge into decision making.

5. Groups Need Leaders

Leadership is measured by a series of different traits and has a significant impact on the experience of people who attend small groups. The more traits a leader has, the more likely it is for an attender to have a powerful experience in their group.

Maximizing Groups

Group life is a resource and a gift to the disciple-making vision of a local church. As your group is pointed in the right direction, led by the right person, made up of the right character, and behaving in the right manner, you now need to reproduce and reproduce often. Don't make the mistake of being content with the groups you have.

Maximize your groups by multiplying your options. Our research on nonattenders provides some valuable insight as to why continuing to create new groups is an important aspect of small-group development. One reason to continue with new classes is that 32 percent of nonattenders stopped participating because the class ended. Basically a third of the people who are no longer involved with groups state that it was because the class ended and there was no desirable alternative—no next step. You need to think about two things: (1) anticipate the needs of those who might be attending, and (2) determine the subsequent session topics.

It is also true that 33 percent of nonattenders do not currently attend because personal responsibilities keep them busy when groups are offered, and 22 percent say the classes or groups meet at an inconvenient time. While recalling that 80 percent of nonattenders are open to or looking for a new class, this information should compel us to consistently start new groups.

Maximize your groups by multiplying leaders. Around half of pastors strongly or moderately agree their church regularly starts new small classes or groups. According to a LifeWay Research survey of a thousand Protestant pastors, the mean number of new, ongoing Bible study groups started in the past year is four while the median is only two. This would seem to indicate that churches are not proactively starting groups in anticipation of what is needed. The pastors were asked to provide the biggest barrier to starting new groups at their church. The most common types of barriers suggested by the pastors were:

- Time; busy; finding the right time (25%)
- Apathy; lack of interest; commitment; participation (22%)
- Lack of leaders or volunteers; trained leaders; willing leaders (17%)

The solution to all three obstacles is the biggest challenge for most churches: finding the right leaders. We challenge you, as we have multiple times in this book, to put as much energy as possible in leadership development. Work on the work instead of in the work by multiplying leaders.

A New Leadership Culture

We insist on reviewing a critical principle as you attempt to create a transformational culture through groups: *Culture is changed by influence, not by control.*

How does this impact your leadership development culture? You have control options. One option is to make each group have an apprentice. Another option is to require groups to multiply after a year. Neither of those is a good option and will do more harm to your culture than good. Rules create mistrust because rules communicate mistrust. You also have influence options. You influence through intentional conversations and relationships. Sound better? You can move a leader's feet by force, or you can move their hearts by influence and inspiration.

How Jesus Called His Leaders

When you take a closer look at how Jesus called His original twelve disciples, you discover some incredibly powerful elements of a multiplication culture. If we took Jesus' team building and leadership development principles out of context, many of us may disagree with them. Some might say His approach was risky or that He set the bar too low. Others may say Jesus was setting Himself up for failure because of the spiritual maturity level of people He chose. Let's watch Jesus lay the foundation for developing His team by implementing five unique grace leadership factors.

He called them before they were believers. This may be uncomfortable for some of us to process—yet Jesus called the disciples to fish for men before they had been caught themselves! Notice what Jesus didn't say to the future disciples: "Invite Me into your heart. I will help you grow and live a better life." He said, "Follow Me, and I will make you into the men I desire you to be." Jesus didn't call disciples; He called lost men!

There is a risky reality when it comes to rapid multiplication of leaders. The vetting process in some church cultures is daunting. And yet from pastoral leadership and beyond, our system of intense scrutiny does not yield perfect results. How many churches have experienced moral failure from their pastors, deacons, elders, and teachers? How does a robust leadership vetting process protect the church from the hearts of men and women who lead them?

Neither can you make a case that Jesus' original twelve disciples were remotely saved, doctrinally prepared, or trained when Jesus invited them to be in His inner circle. He developed them along the way, often questioning whether they had any faith.

Bob Logan puts light to the issue of leadership development with a simple illustration. He said, "Too often we attempt to teach people to swim in a classroom." If you have ever taken swimming lessons, you immediately get the importance of getting in the water and practicing under the watchful eye of a swimming rabbi. Jesus invited the original twelve to go swimming with Him. He was not reducing what was needed to change the world to an intellectual experience in a classroom.

Can you imagine the leadership and relationship bar Jesus set when the community saw His inner circle of followers? The lowest in the community were drawn to Jesus because the lowest in the community knew they had a place. For a tax cheat and liar like Matthew to be in Jesus' inner circle gave great hope for hurting tax cheats and liars. People like Matthew, as well as Peter, John, and others, were the best raw material upon which to create a movement.

What were the Luke 15 people really thinking who were drawn to Jesus? The evidence that they had a potential place close to Jesus was compelling. Jesus was such a respected rabbi with an incredible résumé of welcoming people into His life:

> All the tax collectors and sinners were approaching to listen to Him. And the Pharisees and scribes were complaining, "This man welcomes sinners and eats with them!" (Luke 15:1–2)

What about your inner circle of disciples? What is their spiritual résumé? If it is long-standing and impressive, future disciples may be getting a message you really don't want to send. Your discipleship and multiplication culture may include a silent message of "this is how good you need to be in order to lead and multiply—good luck!"

He sent them before they were ready. The time lapse between Jesus' invitation to follow and fish and new disciple deployment is not easy to proof text or measure. But there is a compelling case that is not very long. From Luke's perspective it took about four chapters to get to that point. How long do you need to begin to trust leaders enough to develop them with hands-on experience?

We, with our best intentions, create a leadership bottleneck in our local churches. The equation looks pretty innocent and in some cases quite noble. We lift a high bar for leadership; we make it clear to all, and everyone gets it. In fact, they may get it all the way to irresponsibility and disobedience. The devil whispers in their ear: "Don't worry, you will never measure up—plus, you don't have time to be so committed."

You may be teaching disciples how not to be disciples. You are communicating that they have a long way to go. At this point in their journey, they should feel no more pressure to lead than they feel to become brain surgeons.

Part of our research revealed something of critical importance to disciple making. We asked what leadership behavior seemed to result in group participants "following Christ more closely." We can argue that if small groups had only one outcome, this one would be the most important. In an ideal situation, service, relationships, and evangelism flow from "following Christ more closely," don't you think?

So, what does this leader who helps people "follow Christ more closely" look like? This leader is "transparent about his or her own weaknesses and struggles," according to attenders in those groups. If we want leaders who are victorious over any struggles and weaknesses, we may not have anyone ready to lead—ever.

The bottom line—Jesus sent His disciples out long before they were ready to do things they had never done before. Their preparation was organic, simple, and painstakingly relational.

In each Gospel disciples were called early in Jesus' ministry. Although knowing the exact chronological progression of the spiritual journeys of the original twelve, we know He moved quickly. The disciples were invited to follow Jesus as early as John 1:35–41 and as late as Luke 5:1–11. From the time these disciples were invited to follow Jesus, how soon were they "sent"? Faster than many of us would be comfortable sending someone.

The conversation around local churches always seems to be, "We just don't have any leaders ready to be on the team." Again, that is a reflection about your belief in the way God shapes people and builds teams. Jesus chose His team and then molded them. His leaders did not come into the job ready-made. Part of their spiritual journey was to be invited to be on a team—often in an underdeveloped stage.

Sending is a critical part of the molding process, but notice how Jesus sent, then debriefed constantly. Too many pastors and staff members don't embrace their role as coaches. They may preach and claim to believe Ephesians 4:12, but in reality they function as ones who do the "the work of ministry." The role that is being ignored is "the training of the saints." The original word for "training" has to do with making sure they are completely and thoroughly equipped with everything they need to accomplish the tasks at hand. This is an ongoing, full-time job.

Pastors and staff who spend all their time doing the work of the ministry, while not equipping others, are not fulfilling a biblical role; they are simply being biblical Christians. To be a biblical Christian is the responsibility of every believer on the planet, and nobody gets financial support to be a biblical Christian. That is what we all signed up for when we decided to follow Jesus Christ. The financial support of the church body comes when you are actively engaged in equipping and training others.

In the Gospel of Mark, for example, the disciples fumbled, bumbled, and fell numerous times in awkward and inexcusable ways, post-sending. And remember, even the Gospels admit we are only getting part of the story—we missed numerous outtakes. According to John, the disciples saw much more than could possibly be written down (John 20:30–31). Our theological speculation would include the fact that they probably said and did many more dumb things, too.

Peter corrected the content of Jesus' teaching (8:31–33). The disciples failed to cast out a demon (9:18–19). The disciples tried to stop someone who was successfully casting out demons (9:38–41). The disciples rebuked people for bringing children to Jesus (10:13–15) and James and John asked for promotion and power (10:38–37).

A significant part of Christ being formed in disciples comes after the sending, not before. Thus, to delay sending is to delay Christ's formation. We have seen this principle in our ministry context lived out continually. And in fact, we have experienced this in our own personal ministry journeys.

He cast vision before they could see. "'Don't be afraid,' Jesus told Simon. 'From now on you will be catching people!' Then they brought the boats to land, left everything, and followed Him" (Luke 5:10–11). How did Jesus possibly know that such ordinary men would be used to change the world? Peter failed in plain sight of Jesus multiple times after this initial invitation. Could Jesus have had second thoughts about His own leadership development process? We might be harder on ourselves than we realize.

We have all had those "What was I thinking?" moments when developing people. Jesus was fully human. I wonder if after Peter initially refused to let Jesus wash his feet, or after Peter cut off Malchus's ear (John 18:10), or after Peter denied Him three times (John 18:15–27) Jesus was tempted to give up on Peter.

As a leadership developer and multiplier, guard your heart against the pride of being wrong about someone. Never let pride cause you not to take a risk on people. Of course, we all want to have the level of discernment that causes us to choose and develop the right people. But caution will never work if you want to multiply leaders rapidly. Jesus picked Judas. We find no evidence that picking Judas embarrassed Jesus. Jesus picked Peter, and we have more embarrassing Peter moments than anyone.

If you have never been wrong about someone, then swallow your pride and get more aggressive in your choices. You are playing too safe if there is never the possibility of failure. Take risks with people. The great group leader in your church may be hiding behind the worst exterior. Practice discernment, but do not allow the potential stumbling to keep you from going out on a limb. If we do not believe God can transform and equip certain individuals to be dynamic leaders, our view of God and His grace is much too small.

Jesus spoke people forward. He had a heart for the world and a heart for cities. But Jesus also demonstrated His heart for individuals. Notice how He spoke into Peter's life before He invested any time in Him. "From now on you will be catching people!" Jesus said.

Right into the lives of common vision fisherman, Jesus predicted the future.

Leaders create a multiplication culture by what they say. "You are not ready yet" is not a wrong thought. But we suggest you create a positive multiplication culture by saying, "One day you will . . ." or, "From now on you will . . ."

Take your children as an example. When your preschool daughter says, "Daddy, I want to be a doctor when I grow up," your response will shape her identity. You would never say, "Are you kidding me? You can't even add 1+1 yet. You can't write your name or color in the lines. I wouldn't trust you as my doctor." Your likely response would be, "And you will be the most wonderful doctor in the world some day."

Humanly speaking, Jesus did not know that Peter would catch men. But Jesus knew the power of the Father to transform people. What we say to people reveals the condition of our hearts. Jesus' optimism about Peter, James, and John was not because He had read a positive-thinking book. What Jesus said to His future disciples revealed what Jesus really believed about the people and the power of His Father.

We have presented this principle throughout Transformational Groups: *Groups are not about groups; they are about disciples.* So the people who populate them must be seen as vast open fields of potential for God to do unusual, supernatural things. You will only create an institutional command and control leaders through doubting people's sincerity.

The Bible presents a clear pattern of God's potential to work in His children. One example is in John's Gospel: "But to all who did receive Him, He gave them the right to be children of God, to those who believe in His name" (John 1:12).

Notice He did the same thing in Acts 1:8 for an entire group of leaders. Watch Jesus predict the future and speak His followers forward:

But you will receive power when the Holy Spirit has come
on you, and you will be My witnesses in Jerusalem, in all
Judea and Samaria, and to the ends of the earth. (Acts 1:8)

He invested before they proved they were worthy. You do not have
to be an NFL fan to know that finding new superstars is the lifeblood
of the league. Each team invests millions to find great players, and
yet their mistakes in assessing potential are common.

The most famous public display of looking for new players is a
four-day event each year called the NFL Scouting Combine. Three
hundred players are invited, tested, and measured to determine who
is worth the investment. The total cost of the event is around 2.5 million dollars.[2]

You know the value of picking the right players for your group
leader team far outweighs the cost. But there is no proven way to
remove all the risk of making investments in people. Sometimes a
player still turns out to be a bust in spite of all the testing and measuring and coaching he received. The people business is often messy
and always unpredictable.

Just ask the NFL coaches and general managers who used their
first-round pick to draft players who became known as "busts." Or
to shift to another sport, think how the Portland Trailblazers in the
NBA felt after they drafted Sam Bowie, who had a mediocre and
injury-plagued career, instead of some kid from the University of
North Carolina named Michael Jordan.

Did you ever wonder what Jesus really saw in the original twelve
disciples that made them worth the investment? We have. It may
help inform us what kind of leaders we will invest our time in.

Conventional wisdom says Jesus saw nothing in them, yet to
assume they were all losers is a big assumption. And it would be irresponsible to think Jesus randomly picked them. Jesus was choosing
an inner circle of leaders, eleven of whom would initiate the entire
Christian movement.

We can only speculate what Jesus saw in them. For Peter it may have been the hard work and persistency as a fisherman. Maybe Andrew's ability to work with teams made an impression. Fishing for a living in that day was not a one-man operation that looked like a lonely guy sitting by himself at the end of a pier.

For Matthew, it may have been the same passion that caused him to invite his friends to a party soon after he met Jesus, or it might have been his analytical skills that helped him count money well.

When Jesus called these men, no matter their natural wiring and abilities, they were raw material in kingdom terms. No matter how good they were, what guarantee did Jesus have that they would understand or fully embrace a gospel that was not yet to be revealed? And yet there was no apparent "Disciple Scouting Combine" to compare one against the other. Jesus chose them, plain and simple, and because He chose them, they were qualified.

Multiplying leaders for the gospel involves risk and investment with no foolproof way to predict outcomes. But everyone is worth the effort and investment. Jesus ultimately proved that as clarified in John 3:16: "For God loved the world in this way: He gave His One and Only Son, so that everyone who believes in Him will not perish but have eternal life."

In spite of the risk, Jesus invested. Rejection and blasphemy followed, but so did transformation. In fact, His original disciples never really proved they were worthy. They ran and denied all the way to the end. What made them worthy? The Holy Spirit, which justifies any investment into people!

He understood that all of them would not be winners. If you have never picked a loser, then you have not made enough decisions. You are guilty of possibly having left the best players on the sideline. Your potential to multiply leaders is lowered. No one should argue that they have never had a disciple disappoint.

When Jesus chose Judas to be a disciple, it was another high-risk choice. Jesus' choice was not a mistake, but the story was far from a leadership development success.

Jesus seemed to have Judas in mind when He said, "But there are some among you who don't believe" (John 6:64). Yet the context was that He was speaking to disciple(s), and He did not say "one" but "some."

The narrative context of Jesus' statement is notable. Jesus had just done two of His greatest natural miracles, feeding the multitudes and walking on water. This led to a group discussion about the source of eternal bread.

The group was confused about what they really wanted—an eternal bread source (now) or a source for eternal bread (later). A great way to assess where a disciple is spiritual is supported by this principle. What do they really want? Something now or something forever? Unlimited temporary help or unlimited eternal life with Jesus? And how are their values transforming from the temporary to the eternal?

Not all of the crowds were genuine disciples, but the dialogue seemed to move to a smaller circle. The disciples, not the crowd, had serious questions to the point that they were talking among themselves. They seemed offended at such teaching, particularly when Jesus referred to His body as bread.

Jesus overheard them. A great disciple maker listens to determine where disciples are in their spiritual development. In fact, a great discipler uses his ears at least as much as he uses his voice. Jesus was a great disciple maker.

Now you see the words and action of Jesus. How much someone fulfills their God-given potential under your leadership is not completely in your control. Whether they become winners or not is not a reflection on you. It is somewhat comforting to know that Jesus had defectors, even from His core group—and He could walk on water!

At times tough disciple-making conversations are critical. This conversation was such that, "From that moment many of His disciples turned back and no longer accompanied Him" (John 6:66). And after those left, Jesus opened the door for the Twelve to leave by saying, "You don't want to go away too, do you?" (John 6:67).

Not all Christ followers are superstars, but this is where our grace stories give God great glory. An incredible closing to this episode, and even more perplexing, was Jesus' comments that included John's editorial:

> Jesus replied to them, "Didn't I choose you, the Twelve? Yet one of you is the Devil!" He was referring to Judas, Simon Iscariot's son, one of the Twelve, because he was going to betray Him. (John 6:70–71)

Jesus did not choose winners; He chose people. He did not choose disciples; He chose mere men and, more than we will ever be able to account for, aborted their journey with Him. If our vision is to multiply groups and leaders, then we can never let pride or making a bad choice cause us to stop imagining a movement. We are in good company with Jesus when we take a chance on people that we are willing to invest our lives to thoroughly equip with everything they need to accomplish the tasks at hand.

Why Multiplication Matters

Community is essential when it comes to successfully living out the Christian walk in a day-to-day context. So the math is simple:

More community = More disciples

Understanding the nature of groups helps you see again their incredible potential for the kingdom.

As culture drifts more and more toward individualism, transformational churches are taking on the responsibility of moving people into authentic relationships with one another, many through groups and classes. The Bible offers illustrations of the need for and benefits of small units of community.

In Exodus 18, Jethro, Moses' father-in-law approached him and said, "What you're doing is not good. You will certainly wear out both yourself and these people" (Exod. 18:17–18). The principle here is applicable for pastors, church leaders, and members: when people do not have small units of connection and relationship, it wears everyone out. The pastors and leaders are constantly working to fulfill that need for connection. The members are unable to be in the nurturing relationships they need. Similarly, small units of community allow people to "carry one another's burdens" (Gal. 6:2) in a way that simply is impossible in larger group settings. Therefore, Scripture favors small settings for accomplishing genuine community.

In addition to scriptural favor toward small units, the institution of small groups addresses significant cultural needs. In *Bowling Alone*, Putnam explains the shift in our culture away from community and toward what some have called "cocooning." As a result of this societal shift, the nuclear family is nuclearized into small units, disconnected from others along the way. However, we believe a shift back toward interpersonal relationships is taking place.

Why is this shift happening in the church? Because small groups are meeting the needs of people to grow in faith by learning in a community with some purpose. We want and need to be connected—it is not good to be alone—so that we can grow and help one another.

Most of these needs can be best met in small groups, where people are able to mature in their faith, as they respect, appreciate, listen to, and hear those in community alongside them. As we are comforted in our affliction, we are able to comfort others in their affliction (2 Cor. 1:4).

Though Christians experience the need for authentic community, they often need nudging to acknowledge and live in the reality of that need. Similarly, many of us understand our need for exercise but require encouragement to participate and, thus, enjoy the benefits! Group life is no different. Our research has shown that people will engage in groups, but with any change in life situation, or even if the class ends, they disappear.

Four Facets of Transformational Groups

In the church setting groups provide an opportunity to encourage people into life-changing community. However, the significance of groups goes beyond the benefits of personal life change and becomes crucial for the transformational church.

Four important facets of groups demonstrate their transformational nature:

1. Connectible

Groups provide the best framework for significant relationships to develop. William Hendricks wrote a book entitled *Exit Interviews*. He interviewed some of the thousands of people who leave the church each week and never come back. *One of the key reasons people left was their* **failure to connect** *with other people in relationships.* They found that a lot of people were already established and connected and not naturally open to welcoming them into their "circles." If your church is going to be transformational, it needs to be a place where the stranger can connect significantly.

2. Reproducible

In human growth, multiplication allows the cell to become multiple cells, which allow change and growth to occur. Similarly, for growth to occur in the church, people groups must continuously grow and multiply. Smaller groups are more easily multiplied than larger groups.

Smaller groups are easy to reproduce, much more so than a large-group experience. It's not rocket science. People have been preaching this for years. Arthur Flake, the well-known Sunday school expert in the 1900s, actually created a formula and strategy for church growth through Sunday school growth almost one hundred years ago.

Flake's plan was pretty simple (and that was the genius of it). He was not seminary trained and just claimed to be an organizer. His plan was simple:

- Know the possibilities.
- Enlarge the organization.
- Provide the space.
- Enlist and train the workers.
- Go after the people.[3]

His idea was that if you started more groups and enlisted more leaders, then people would be reached. His ideas launched a movement—at one point, Sunday schools were larger than churches, partly because of the influence and ideas of people like Flake and the multiplication focus he had.

As Flake displayed, groups must be multiplied. We believe such groups will increasingly be key environments for evangelism today. Large-group evangelistic meetings were very prominent in the 1950s, but apart from a few exceptions, mass-evangelism has largely given way to smaller group evangelism in today's culture. (Witness the global explosion of resources like The Alpha Course, which has more than fifteen million people going through the course in small groups, or Christianity Explored, and many others.)

People don't invite their friends to a "crusade" as much today as they would to their group. New Christians will be multiplied in groups, and consequently the church will grow.

3. Assimilative

Just as groups connect newcomers to the church through relationships, groups assimilate people to ministry through service. As people in groups grow in relationship together, they will readily serve alongside others and integrate into ministry opportunities.

Groups enhance assimilation. Along these same lines, assimilation and transformation are great motivators for group establishment. When someone has connected with new friends over the first six months, they are statistically more likely not only to attend but also to get involved at that church for the long-term.

As previously mentioned, that's a lot harder to accomplish in the context of a large group. What's more, when people who have not yet received Jesus as their Savior do become assimilated into a group community, they are asking questions and wrestling with answers along with others who are doing the same thing. When they do actually make that decision to follow Christ, transformation tends to be deeper and faster in that setting.

4. Transferable

Groups can be excellent ways to start churches. As an essential element of the transformational church, church planting generally necessitates a core group of people who are sent out to reach a new area.

Groups are one of the most effective strategies for church planting. In Ed's own experience, while pastoring a church in Erie, Pennsylvania, they simply sent out two of their healthiest and strongest groups into two different communities and blessed them to start a new church there. The smaller group naturally became the core group for the new church and was a natural next step for each group.

Groups provide your church with an opportunity to connect people in genuine relationships. Through interpersonal relationships, group members will experience life change as they fulfill their need for community in an individualistic society. Ultimately, as groups grow and multiply, so will the church. And as the church grows, gospel influence multiplies in your community.

Multiplication matters because people matter. And at the end of the day, there is a vision that should drive the dissatisfaction with our current realities. The vision does not come from us. Neither does it come from well-known speakers. The vision comes from God Himself through His servant in exile, John:

> After this I looked, and there was a vast multitude from
> every nation, tribe, people, and language, which no one
> could number, standing before the throne and before the

Lamb. They were robed in white with palm branches in their hands. (Rev. 7:9)

We see more than our churches growing with groups and impacting our communities. What drives maximizing the groups, or any other thing we do for God, is the "vast multitude from every nation, tribe, people, and language."

Rick Howerton (discipleship and small groups consultant for LifeWay) has, as his life mission statement, to see "a biblical small group within walking distance of every person on the planet making disciples that make disciples." He sincerely believes that, if biblical groups will multiply, in time the world will hear and embrace the gospel, and the masses will become followers of Jesus Christ.

I wonder, would your church and your group leaders embrace a dream of this nature and make it your goal to have a biblical group within walking distance of every person in your town or city?

From the Group

Because of my small group, I'm more open to others and care more about their concerns. I find myself talking to God more and praying for others more often. This has definitely drawn me closer to God. Groups can make you feel like you belong to the family of God.

—Donna

What Now?

- What is your strategy for multiplying group leaders?
- What major change can you make to multiply leaders faster?

8
Connect with Disconnected People

> *While earlier generations of Americans*
> *were permanent residents attached to a place, we are*
> *nomads, perpetual immigrants condemned to move*
> *from place to place in our own country.*
> —David Wells[1]

Next Step: *Connect with disconnected people for transformational groups.*

Longtime Christians, Denny and Dede moved into a new neighborhood in a new city to take a new job. They did not have any family or friends in the area, but they understood biblical community. They decided to get to know the neighbors. It was a newer community so the other residents were not rooted so strongly they could not breach. Every night they sat outside on their front porch. Neighbors started waving and then started talking from the sidewalk as they passed by with dogs and kids. Those conversations made their way to the driveway and finally sitting on the porch sipping lemonade on a warm evening.

Before long, Denny and Dede started learning the names of their neighbors. Every time neighbors introduced themselves, Dede wrote their names down. They took special note of children's names and even dog's names. Cats were ignored, although one neighbor had a pet hedgehog!

Walks in the neighborhood were often interrupted by conversations with neighbors. Denny and Dede even grilled dinner with their neighbors, Tim and Amanda. This was the first time they had a meal with any neighbor, ever. The conversation was casual, but a connection was made.

Denny made an effort to help this young, hardworking couple by mowing their lawn, helping with errands around Tim's house, and being a good neighbor. Denny had no agenda except to image the gospel to his neighbors.

One night Denny took his dog out for a walk and saw Tim and Amanda with their young son. Tim immediately shared his burden from his day at work. This was a first. Tim apologized for blurting out but continued, nonetheless, to unload his burden. Amanda added her struggles of working full-time, being a mother of a toddler, and her recent health issues.

Out of the blue Tim asked Denny where he went to church. Tim explained his church experience that ended badly when he asked the minister to perform a ceremony for him and Amanda, who was pregnant. That was two years ago, and he had not been back to church since. Amanda said her church experience was worse. She went to church with her grandparents who let on like they were holy but secretly lived a life not consistent with Scripture. Amanda had not been to church for over twenty years.

Tim and Amanda are not an isolated case. They are one of many disconnected families in your neighborhoods and cities. We don't know if Tim and Amanda would have found a church on their own, but in any case Denny and Dede's efforts to make themselves available to their neighbors helped connect a couple back to the local body where we pray transformation will never end.

"We are nomads, perpetual immigrants," David Wells reminded us (see LeaderSpeak quote above). More transplanted residents live in isolation among one another, all wishing silently for a little friendship. The Bible refers to connecting to one another as "hospitality." Hospitality was a common characteristic of first-century Christianity.

> After she [Lydia] and her household were baptized, she urged us, "If you consider me a believer in the Lord, come and stay at my house." And she persuaded us [disciples]. (Acts 16:15)

> The local people showed us extraordinary kindness, for they lit a fire and took us all in, since it was raining and cold. (Acts 28:2)

> For I was hungry and you gave Me something to eat; I was thirsty and you gave Me something to drink; I was a stranger and you took Me in. (Matt. 25:35)

> Share with the saints in their needs; pursue hospitality. (Rom. 12:13)

We want to explore some ideas about connecting to disconnected people, first among those who attend a church gathering and, second, in your neighborhoods.

Five Ways to Connect with Disconnected People in the Church

Church members need to find opportunities to connect with disconnected people that attend the church gathering. People need to be assimilated into the church fairly quickly. If people do not get plugged into some meaningful community within six months of their attending a church, they almost always drop out. It may be more like six weeks in our instant-gratification culture. If they do get assimilated, they are probably going to stick, and that opens up doors for evangelism, discipleship, and spiritual transformation not only for them and their family but also for their extended family and friends.

People come to a church gathering, and they will typically visit anonymously to check things out. They are looking for a connection to God that comes through worship, prayer, the sermon, and Communion. They are also looking for a connection to people; otherwise they would stay at home and watch an Internet church. If they connect with God at the gathering but don't connect with people, they may miss an opportunity for their spiritual growth, health, and sometimes their spiritual birth. Let's look at five ways a church body can connect with the disconnected.

1. Take Advantage of the Three-Minute Rule

The three-minute rule begins when the final prayer is said or song is sung. This is not the time to talk to your best friends. During those first three minutes, two things are going to happen: people who are familiar are going to talk to one another, and people who don't know anybody are going to leave *quickly*. This is where it's crucial.

If you take the time to talk to the people in those first three minutes who aren't connected, you will have time afterward to talk to your friends who are more likely to stick around. You need to see those first three minutes after a church gathering as a time-sensitive corporate fishing pond for group prospects and for showing Christian hospitality. You have three critical minutes to look immediately around for people who are not connected in the body. Be friendly to them and ask them if they are in a group and invite them if they are not connected to one.

2. Make Yourself Available as a Group Leader

People who are not connected will often slip out after the sermon, sometimes during the prayer. It is not surprising that they don't excitedly anticipate the offering and closing benediction. Key group leaders should move to the exit areas to connect with the disconnected right after the sermon. The people who are the most disconnected will exit before they have to speak to anyone. They may not be ready to connect, but you can at the least be a friendly face on their way out. If they return, you will have a greater opportunity to connect them to a group when they are ready.

3. Know Where the Groups Meet and Have a Groups Concierge in a Prime Location

As a group leader trying to connect with newer people, know what groups may work best for the person you are trying to connect. If the visiting family lives fifteen miles east of the church gathering, asking them to attend a group that meets fifteen miles west would not seem very responsible to expect them to drive sixty miles round-trip every week for a group meeting. Try to connect them with a group that meets fairly close to their home. If you are not sure, walk over to the groups counter with them and help them find one that best suits them. You can offer your assistance based on their demographic or their interests as well as your knowledge of the leaders. The goal is connecting them to a group that best serves their needs, not that best serves your need to have a larger sized group.

4. Invite Them to a Basic Newcomers' Class or Informal Gathering

Connect with people by inviting them to a basic newcomers' gathering. This could be a class that highlights the foundations of your church, or it could be an informal gathering that helps them find their next steps for assimilating into the church. Design this as an opportunity for them to connect with other people such as group leaders, key leaders, and pastors. The goal of this newcomers' gathering is to connect them with the mission and vision of the church, with other people, and with a group.

5. Follow Up

Here is where we go old school. Many churches have abandoned some basic follow-up of visitors to their church gatherings. Below are some follow-up things we do.

- Provide the names and contact information of people who attend the newcomers' gathering to group leaders. We want group leaders to connect them to a group as soon as possible.
- Call visitors on the phone on Sunday night to thank them for visiting.
- The church mails out a typed letter on Monday.
- The lead pastor can send visitors a handwritten note on Thursday. It is a short note. At Ed's church the letter reads, "Thank you for being our guest this Sunday at Grace Church. We hope you were challenged and encouraged. Please let us know if you have any questions or if we can be of service in any way. God bless, Ed Stetzer."
- An optional follow-up is really old school. Stop by their house with a baked good. This may work better in some parts of the country than in others.
- Have a group leader contact and invite them the next week.

We want to move disconnected people who are sitting in rows toward becoming connected people who are sitting in circles. If we do that quickly, they're almost certain to stay and become connected into the life of our church. If they're not yet believers, they're going to hear the gospel in the context of having some friends around them, and that is the ultimate goal. We want them in the kingdom and not just in the building. It starts with a simple connection.

Not everyone you can connect with is in your church. Below are six suggestions for connecting with your neighbors. Every host family should pay close attention to some of these ideas. Regardless, you may connect with a disconnected family like Tim and Amanda.

Six Ways to Connect to Your Disconnected Neighbors

Jesus said to love our neighbors as we love ourselves (Matt. 22:39). The problem is that many of us don't even know our neighbors. The command to love our neighbors is not just a theoretical concept. It is a choice to take action. It can be strategically planned with a little forethought to sincerely show them and tell them about the One who loves them infinitely. You can demonstrate love to your neighbors in six ways.

1. Get to Know Your Neighbors

Choose eight to ten houses near your residence to pray for, minister, and have spiritual conversations. If you live in the woods somewhere, apply these principles to your coworkers. Get to know your neighbors by name. Know their kids' names and their dogs' names. You can ignore the cats; they are, no doubt, ignoring you. Look for opportunities to be Christlike: love, grace, mercy, sacrifice, and serve. Your approach toward them is not to close a business deal; you are walking with them in their spiritual journey. Be sure to celebrate their baby steps along the way.

2. Reach Out to Each of Them Monthly

Make a list of your neighbors, and try to do something to reach out to each of them at least once a month. Look for ways to serve them. Make yourself available to your neighbors, even if they are resistant to Christianity. I (Ed) was exercising on the elliptical when our doorbell rang. I answered the door with my sweat dripping all over a teenage boy in the neighborhood. They were not overly responsive to the gospel, but, in spite of that, the teenage son asked me if I could explain to him what it meant to be a Christian. Why did he and his parents come to my house? I think he came to me because I had consistently reached out to him and his family and had built a relationship.

3. Pray for Your Neighbors

Commit to praying for your neighbors. Walk the neighborhood and ask God for open opportunities to talk to them about spiritual things. Pray for their protection and for their children. You might even ask them what things you could specifically pray about for their family. God will begin to increase your love for them as you consistently pray for them.

4. Invite Your Neighbors to Your Group or Church

Some people would not think of attending a church service but would gladly go to a small-group meeting where you were either hosting or attending. If they are already active in a local church, affirm them. If they are not, those are the neighbors you can pursue spiritually. This may seem basic, but people are more responsive when someone with whom they have a relationship has invited them to church. They may be waiting for an invitation. Remember, 80 percent said they would be open to attend a group if asked.

5. Be Present in the Neighborhood

Make yourself present in the neighborhood. When neighbors are outside, sit on your front porch, not on your back deck. Join them wherever they are mingling. Take your kids or dogs for a walk with the intention of meeting the neighbors. Go with your family to parks and recreation areas near your neighborhood. Participate in as many neighborhood meetings and events as you are able. Patronize establishments near your home, especially in an urban setting.

6. Have a Neighborhood Party

Jesus was comfortable at parties. His first miracle was performed at a wedding when He turned water into wine. He was a friend of publicans and sinners. We need to learn how to be comfortable around people who do not necessarily share or practice our same values. Jesus did not come to call the righteous to repentance. Throw (fun) parties in your neighborhoods as a way to connect the disconnected.

Group-Sponsored Events

With a little forethought and planning, your family and small group could host an event in your neighborhood with the intent of being on mission together. The members of your group can assist you. They may get some ideas for what it means to live on mission in a community. Below are five ideas for connecting with neighbors through group-sponsored events. You can come up with many others that work best in your community.

1. Fireworks Display

We (Ed) have hosted the neighborhood fireworks display for several years. It might have been illegal, but we did it all for the glory of God! Our neighbors gathered together and watched the fireworks. It was a great opportunity to meet people we did not know.

2. Pool Party

You can host a pool party where you invite people in the neighborhood. Grill some meat and invite some of the neighbors you do not know. Be sure to provide sunscreen, towels, and lots of water.

3. Block Party

A church planter recently tweeted a picture of his neighborhood block party in the upper west side of Manhattan. It was encouraging to see this because if it can be done in Manhattan, it can be done anywhere. A block party is a fun event where all of the neighbors are invited. Your group can help facilitate one for every member of your group that lives in a neighborhood. It is not that hard to do.

In some cities a citywide push on a specific night acts as a "night out against crime." You could use this civic push to host your block party. In fact, if you register your National Night Out block party online, they will send you a free NNO Organizational Kit filled with how-to materials.[2] You can also do a block party on a holiday, like Labor Day or Memorial Day or Fourth of July or any day that works best for your neighborhood. The neighbors could participate by bringing food or beverages. You could provide inflatable bounce houses. Kids will beg their parents to go, and you will make key connections with many of your neighbors.

4. Halloween

We are aware that some Christians do not like to participate in Halloween observations. I (Ed) do and I will tell you why. This is the one night in the year when people will actually come to your house and introduce themselves to you. Your (Christian) home should have the best candy. You can easily stay away from the occult connections and redeem the holiday as an opportunity to reach (and treat) your neighbors.

5. Welcome to the Neighborhood

As new people move into your neighborhood, they are open to receiving a welcome from you with something like cookies. You might even consider including some sugar-free and nut-free and gluten-free items for those with dietary restrictions. You could deliver these on a group night to show how easily this is done.

A transformational group is a group that connects with God, with members of the group, and with those who are disconnected—in the church and in our neighborhoods. It starts with transformed disciples who are following Jesus—in community.

"Follow Me," He told them, "and I will make you fish for people!" (Matt. 4:19)

From the Group

I never considered going back to church. We were burned a few times and were the recipients of judgment and condemnation. It just wasn't worth it. When our daughter was born, we started reconsidering church. I did not know where to start looking, and then I found out my neighbor was a Christian. He encouraged us to attend his church. We are going to try again this Sunday.

—Tim

What Now?

- What strategies do you need to implement to connect disconnected people in your church?
- What changes can you make to influence groups to connect to people in their neighborhoods?

9
Imagine the Possibilities

LeaderSpeak

> *Large movements start from small beginnings. If we*
> *plant the right DNA of the kingdom, the growth of the*
> *kingdom is inevitable.*
> —Steve Smith, T4T[1]

Next Step: *Imagine the possibilities.*

Tom and Suzanne lead a group. But it was only two years earlier that Suzanne walked into a group for the first time:

On my way to my first group meeting, I was thinking, What are these people going to be like? Are they going to start calling me "Sister Suzanne"? What if I think they are strange or if they think I am strange? What if they figure out I don't know anything about the Bible? I didn't even own a Bible. . . . I wanted to turn around and go home. That first meeting was very odd, but I left thinking that I needed to buy my own Bible and find out who this person "Ruth" was that they were studying about. I was amazed at how it felt more like a family gathering than a group meeting. I wanted to go back. The following meeting I brought my own Bible with me, and in the following weeks I actually spoke out loud in the group. A lady came up to me and said how she loved it when I spoke and was encouraged by my words. Little by little, I became comfortable enough to share my thoughts and questions. And soon after that, someone told my husband and me that one day we would lead a group.

God used Suzanne's group experience to put her spiritual growth on the fast track. "Because of the biblical community of a group, I have learned how to love, forgive, serve, and give generously." The relationships with the other members of the group helped her apply what she learned through Scripture about how to treat people and how to become someone who builds bridges for others in order to bring them closer to God.

But Suzanne's backstory is even more amazing. She emigrated with her parents from Budapest, Hungary, in 1972 to a refugee camp on Long Island. She was raised in Ohio in a dysfunctional home environment. Suzanne grew up to be an angry and disappointed adult who struggled with relationships, including those with her own children. She felt misunderstood and lacked purpose. Then she had a transformational experience. Suzanne described what happened next: "I walked into church on April 12, 2009, feeling alone, overwhelmed, angry, and lost. I had no idea who Jesus was, who the Holy Spirit was, nor did I own a Bible. Four years later my relationship with God is eternal, Jesus is my friend, and the Holy Spirit dwells inside of me."

God took Suzanne's fear of attending a group and turned it into a critical step of obedience. More steps came in the years following, including leading a group with her husband, Tom. "God has made me a better person, a better mother, a better wife, a better friend."

Her husband Tom is astounded by "seeing the transformation in Suzanne and how she has opened up to use her gifts for mentoring others. She has become an amazing prayer warrior and godly counselor because of doing life with others in groups."

The miraculous part of Suzanne's story goes well beyond her dramatic encounter with Christ that led her daughter to say, "This woman who sits next to me is not the mother who raised me. . . . This is my new mom." God recreated Suzanne into a person who pours into others through groups. God didn't make merely a convert out of Suzanne but a disciple-making disciple.

You know people with stories like Suzanne's. God has placed them in front of you to remind you not only of His ability to convert people but also to make disciple-making disciples. Even beyond that the story reminds us of what God really wants. What does God want me to do? is the wrong question. That question immediately gives you permission to limit God's work to your ability. The right question is this: What does God want?

Use Your Imagination

Most agree the marketing slogan "Imagine the possibilities" began with Apple's introduction of the Intel microchip for the iMac. But a quick Google search reveals that the slogan has moved far beyond Apple. "Imagine the Possibilities" describes everything from life coaching and a nonprofit organization to the Canadian province of Quebec and NASA. Even Apple rival Samsung has used "Imagine" and "Imagine the possibilities" as marketing taglines. Permission to use our imagination is attractive to those of us stuck in patterns of current reality.

The family of God has lost much of its imagination and perhaps needs to listen to the idea of Arthur Flake and "know the possibilities." Of all people, Christ followers should be the last to lose our imagination when we serve the God who spoke an elaborate universe into existence. Maybe it is because we are losing the statistical battle for the American soul, or maybe we have become too distracted to put all our energy into the mission of God. But something has caused us to become realists at best and cynics at worst. Your attitude will affect your groups.

When church leaders think about innovation or creativity, the thinking is typically directed toward the weekend worship gatherings. Entire conferences are devoted to infusing church with creativity and innovation. And while we agree that our God is creative and His followers have the liberty to be creative, isn't limiting our creative thinking to Sunday gatherings a bit ironic. Creativity and innovation should be unleashed in our models of reproduction, our group structures, our intentionality for connecting the unconnected. Surely creativity is not limited to attractional techniques.

Our imaginative creativity should be based on what we know about what God wants and what God thinks about people. Our God has proven Himself over and over again to have no limits when it comes to transformation. When you read Suzanne's story, I hope it helps you imagine the possibilities within your own community. People like Suzanne live near us and near you, too—people who are lost and angry. If we are all really honest, there are times when we wonder whether the gospel can change the most difficult people.

But we read stories and see them firsthand. And then we are reminded that the power of transformation is not inherently resting in a group strategy or any other kind of strategy but in the gospel. A group only becomes the environment God uses (He has proven that), but the gospel is where the power lies (Rom. 1:16).

When we hear and see transformation represented by real lives and faces, we move beyond rhetoric and strategic dialogue and begin to beg God to do this in our communities. We think, "God, that's it. That's what we are so hungry for—that You would powerfully and dramatically shake our communities and cities now. Glorify Yourself through viral responses to the gospel—responses happening in such a way that disciples would make disciples so quickly that a movement takes place."

The Bible said it first: "Now to Him who is able to do above and beyond all that we ask or think according to the power that works in us" (Eph. 3:20). Other versions use the word "imagine" to translate the Greek word *noeo*, which describes an intellectual process rather than an emotional process. Often we will describe something as "hard to wrap our minds around," and that is the spirit of what is being talked about here by Paul to the Ephesians. The picture encourages us to think with our minds—not feel with feelings—about what God could possibly do. In this technology-crazy world, imagine something much more amazing than a microchip.

Imagine a missionary God who wants to restore the "movement" to Christianity in a faster and more dramatic way—superabundantly more than we can "wrap our minds around."

If you think of ten, God is thinking of ten thousand. If you think ten million, God is thinking 100,000,000. He is more than one step ahead of us. So imagine the possibilities, let Scripture inform your dreams, and give your people permission to do the same.

How could God find the Suzannes in your community and revolutionize their existence? God is not limited to "just" saving people but is in the business of immediately changing them into disciple-making disciples. Can you imagine how fast this took place in Suzanne's life? The next time you walk into a crowded store or restaurant in your community, look around. Imagine the whole room as your next group of disciple makers—not just converts or church attenders.

- Imagine a higher number of people in your groups than attends your church on Sunday mornings.
- Imagine viral discipleship.
- Imagine a great movement of leaders developed to shepherd others.
- Imagine groups that care for one another as the early church did.
- Imagine groups that are deeply burdened for their communities.

- Imagine local neighborhoods that rejoice that small groups gather in those neighborhoods because the neighborhoods benefit from the community of faith.
- Imagine local schools being blessed through the missional impulses of small groups.
- Imagine entire cities transformed through smaller communities of Christ followers.

By all means, when you pull out a piece of paper and creatively brainstorm, don't limit your creative juices to a sermon series or cool illustration. Give your best energy to community and toward developing leaders of these ministries that only God can imagine.

God's Ability

Understanding God's potential in your community, city, and region of the world is the prerequisite for a movement. And fully embracing the fact that your church can be on the ground floor of a movement is exciting because that is what He wants. But have you possibly given up on your church too? We challenge you to imagine the possibilities.

When I (Eric) first moved Kaye to Miami, her parents were a bit worried about her living there. She grew up in a small town in North Louisiana with one flashing light, so Miami was a big deal. *CSI Miami* and *Miami Vice* were their impressions, so I promised I would do my best to be sure she was safe and happy. When we bought a house in Homestead, I was so proud to tell my in-laws that their daughter would be living in a gated community so they could rest easy at night.

The gate in our community turned out to be nothing more a mechanical device that looked like a skinny arm with no guard. The arm was nothing more than a big piece of PVC pipe. As if this was not bad enough, the gate was also quickly broken off. In my two and a half years of living there, the gate was only up for approximately forty-two hours.

Here is what happened: people who never received the electronic gate openers or who lost them decided to just run through the gate. They rammed their cars into the PVC-pipe-wannabe-gate and snapped it off. The Homeowners Association would then call and get someone out to fix the gate, and it would be up for a few more hours. And then someone else would run through the gate. This happened several times, and finally the association stopped paying. So the gate in my "gated community" looks unimpressive to anyone who might like to go past it for the wrong reasons.

The gates were no match for cars and thus have been knocked down many times. They were incapable of stopping cars from barreling through. PVC could not stop the movement of a car and its forward momentum. The gates of Hades are no more of a challenge for the church than that PVC pipe was for my neighbor's truck.

The Church's Invincibility

Jesus refers to the church in only two places in the Gospels: in Matthew 16 and 18. Both times He used the word *ekklesia*, which means the "called-out ones." He used "ones" with an "s" because church is never about the individual, only about the community of believers.

In one passage we see the promise He gives concerning the church, and in the other we see a prescription He gives His church for dealing with sin (Matt. 18). The outward challenge (or mission) is answered with a promise. The inward challenge (or sin that negates the mission) is answered with a prescription. These two passages are linked not only because Jesus is speaking in both, but they also contain similar language and imagery that Jesus uses only in these two passages.

Jesus speaks of gates in Matthew 16 when giving a promise about the church. The gates He speaks of are called the gates of Hades, or death. And Jesus says that the gates of Hades, just like the weak gate of my community, are unable to stop the forward movement and the forward momentum of the church. Death and all the forces of evil have the same weakness as a plastic pipe standing in front of a fast-moving Hummer. The things that intimidate us most in life—evil and death—are no match for the church.

Caesarea Philippi was a region filled with idols, shrines, and immoral worship practices. Caesarea Philippi was located near an enormous cave. Many people at that time believed the mouths of caves were entrances to the underworld. They believed caves led down to the abyss, to death, to Hades. So this conversation occurred in a completely pagan area with a cave nearby that some believed was the entrance to Hades and evil:

> When Jesus came to the region of Caesarea Philippi, He asked His disciples, "Who do people say that the Son of Man is?" And they said, "Some say John the Baptist; others, Elijah; still others, Jeremiah or one of the prophets." "But you," He asked them, "who do you, say that I am?" Simon Peter answered, "You are the Messiah, the Son of the living God!" And Jesus responded, "Simon son of Jonah, you are blessed because flesh and blood did not reveal this to you, but My Father in heaven. And I also say to you that you are Peter, and on this rock I will build My church." (Matt. 16:13–18)

Two similar words are used here: "Peter" and "this rock"—but the difference is huge (literally). The word in this text for Peter is *petros*, which means "a small stone or piece of a larger stone." Scholars debate whether Jesus was commending Peter when calling him *petros* or was actually acknowledging Peter's lack of dependability and strength.

The word in this passage for "rock" is *petra*, which means "massive rock." This is even more intriguing because there is an enormous rock at Caesarea Philippi that dwarfs the mighty cave. Imagine the visual lesson as you stand with Jesus and He emphasizes the power of building on the rock in the face of "the gates of hell." Nothing in the passage is meant to make Peter the foundation of Christ's church. In fact, the opposite is being communicated. You can't build anything great on a small piece of gravel. But you can build plenty on a massive, living rock!

Jesus said to Peter, "You are *petros*, you are a small stone, but you did get one thing right." Peter's great declaration reflects this one right thing: "You are the Messiah, the Son of the living God." Jesus said to Peter: "On this rock I will build My church." Thus, "Peter, you are small and weak, but I am massive and strong."

Notice that Jesus says, "I will build My church." I know we all believe, preach, and teach that Jesus is the church builder and that the church belongs to Him. But practically we don't always live and lead like we believe this.

What Is Your Role?

We are deeply concerned about pastors who are working themselves and their families into a dark place. We care that some leaders seem to think they are the only person who stands between people in their community and hell. They do not trust or empower their leaders because they lack confidence in them. So they live on a deserted island or under a juniper tree, believing that everything rises and falls on them and their unique gifts.

Restless and anxious, they pace like a lion—wondering what is the next move to make, staff member to fire or hire, and program to embrace that will help them succeed. They go to bed late and get up early, abusing their bodies and hurting their families.

When we act that way, we are communicating how little we value the work of Christ. We are saying the only way the church can do anything is through my sacrificing my life to make it happen. Why would you think that? Why are you dying for the church? Jesus already did that, and His work is sufficient.

We call for a revival of faith among our pastors whom we deeply love and respect. You are not church builders! He is! We are just gravel on the road to the kingdom. He is a massive rock that is the foundation under the road. How is that for potential? Imagine those possibilities. Review Jesus' statement below and circle key words and phrases that will serve as reminders of His greatness:

> I will build My church, and the forces of Hades will not overpower it. I will give you the keys of the kingdom of heaven, and whatever you bind on earth is already bound in heaven, and whatever you loose on earth is already loosed in heaven. (Matt. 16:18–19)

Jesus said He was going to unleash a movement that would be so powerful and intense that it would be impossible to stop. Our choice seems clear—we can build His church His way or our way. His way sounds so much more remarkable. This great movement is fueled by the power of Jesus on the platform of the *ekklesia*—the living, breathing church. This movement is in transformed people and is fully alive and growing.

By now you may have heard the story of a pastor in Asia named Ying Kai. He had a heart to see God transform his people. His church was responsible for planting one new church a year and was considered to be successful in reaching people. Although he estimated that he and his wife, Grace, were responsible for leading forty to sixty people a year to Christ, this was very little in an area of twenty million people. A restlessness inside Ying kept him searching and dissatisfied.

Ying and Grace were invited to a four-week training class that influenced a new mind-set and approach. But a sign on the wall might have influenced them just as much as the training: "How many of My people will hear the gospel today?" Ying Kai described his breakthrough moment:

> What did Jesus invite His followers to become? Disciples.
> Not simply church members. A disciple must learn
> everything that his teacher teaches him. Then he needs

to follow and to teach other people. My previous way of doing things was different. As a pastor, I had hoped for my congregation to double in size, but that's not what Jesus commanded.[2]

The story of Pastor Ying Kai didn't stop with a new mind-set. The documented results are hard to wrap our minds around but give us permission to imagine the possibilities. Beginning in the year 2000 with a group of thirty people, they began to train the trainers or to essentially view everyone in their small groups as trainers.

After the first full year, through those thirty people, they estimated that 908 groups or "house churches" were started and that more than twelve thousand people were baptized. By 2008, the power of God had produced more than eighty thousand churches and more than two million baptisms. Imagine the possibilities!

Just as the gate in my community could not overcome the power of cars, the gates of death and the evil powers of Satan cannot overcome the church. Ying Kai's story is only one example. But we fear we have lost our imagination in the body of Christ. The gates of hell are powerless to contain the movement of the gospel. And Satan himself is terrified by one thing only—people who have been supernaturally transformed by the gospel.

Jesus told His disciples that He was going to give them the keys to the kingdom of heaven. When someone is given the keys to the city, it is a representation of trust and authority granted, but that does not mean the recipients own the city. Jesus said He is going to entrust them (us) with this movement and they (we) are going to participate in pushing the movement forward.

Jesus used some common rabbi language of binding and loosing to further indicate the authority they would have. Rabbis had the responsibility to declare if something was bound or loosed based on God's standard revealed in the law. If something was bound, it was not permitted. If something was loosed, it was permitted. The language in the passage indicates that the disciples had the authority to declare something bound or loosed based on what has already been decided in heaven.

In these verses Jesus gives authority to the disciples and invites them to participate in the movement of the church. And He asks us to participate in this unstoppable movement as well. Maybe you have missed what we are trying to say:

The movement of the church is unstoppable, and we are invited to participate.

Sometimes we think we are invincible and unstoppable, but those thoughts are killing us and slowing the movement. A story is told about Muhammad Ali on an airplane. The stewardess asked him to put on his seat belt. He said, "I am the greatest of all time. Superman don't need no seat belt." The stewardess said in reply, "Superman don't need no airplane."

We are not unstoppable, but the movement we are part of is. The gates of Hades will not overcome the church. Despite all the stupid things Christians say or do, regardless of all the embarrassing things that may happen within the church, and independent of any scandal or misdirected church leader, the movement of the church is unstoppable.

The gates of Hades will not stop the church. Gates are always defensive. They guard by locking people in or out. But gates never attack, nor are they offensive weapons. The broken gate in my former neighborhood never attacked me, despite all that I have said about it. A gate is incapable of doing so.

Hades is always on the defensive. However, the movement of the church is never on defense. We are always on offense. We always have the ball. There are no defenders on our squad. This is good news. Victory is guaranteed.

The Finish Line

In 1916, the Georgia Tech Engineers squared off against the Cumberland Bulldogs in what would turn out to be a historic football game. John Heisman, for whom the famous award is named, coached Georgia Tech at the time and had arranged a scheduling agreement with Cumberland that would require the school to pay the equivalent of over $63,000 if the Bulldogs failed to show up for the game. Cumberland had cancelled its football program a year earlier but because of the agreement was forced to pull together a team of fourteen to take the field.

Heisman, who also coached baseball at Georgia Tech, believed Cumberland had used professional baseball players masquerading as college students when they crushed the Engineers 22–0 earlier in the year. This led Heisman to show no mercy on the Bulldogs. Before the end of the first quarter, Georgia Tech held a 63–0 lead. They went on to destroy the ragtag Cumberland squad 222–0, the most lopsided game in the history of college football.

When Cumberland took the field that day, there was little doubt what the outcome would be. They never even managed a first down. Oddly enough, neither did Georgia Tech. The difference was that Georgia Tech scored a touchdown on virtually every play from scrimmage. They were simply too much for the Bulldogs.

Believe it or not, the church is in the same position but in some ways even better. The question is not whether the movement we are a part of is going to win. Christ has promised the victory. In fact, the enemy never even gets the ball. The kingdom of darkness is stuck on defense. The question is this: How much will we win by? How big of a dent in the gates of Hades will we make? Will we run up the score? Will we participate in such a way that the movement of the gospel will be advanced powerfully in our communities? The church is unstoppable, but it can still be weakened.

So what could possibly stop the church from storming the gates of hell to thwart Satan's mission? The gates cannot stop the movement and mission of God, but we can stop ourselves. As we end this book, we don't view this as the finish line of just another book. We hope that for you it is the starting point of a new focus on God's transformational mission.

We hope you will approach this starting point with a new sense of confidence in the power of God and the platform of His *ekklesia*. Where do groups fit in? As a biblical arm of the *ekklesia* that provides the best possible environment for true transformation. But the fact that groups exist is not transformational any more than the fact that a local church exists. The product of both—changed lives—is what validates their existence.

What Satan hates is the viral influence of transformed people colaboring with God to reproduce themselves over and over again. People believe people more than they believe ideas. And no matter how restricted or guarded other people can be by laws or by choice from hearing the gospel, a person transformed by God can penetrate any barrier.

Satan can argue with our theology and debate our real intentions. Our obsession with good works can be dismissed with one moral failure in the life of a high-profile spiritual leader. And the poor, even Jesus said, will always be with us (Matt. 26:11), so in spite of our best efforts, the local church will not eradicate poverty. But Satan cannot do anything with a life radically put back together by Jesus.

Jesus gathered these transformed people He put back together and called them "church." And this church would become an unstoppable transformational force in culture. Jesus talked about "church" rarely, but His insight in Matthew 16 is worth reviewing for those of us who are seeking to imagine the possibilities again.

Do These Things

Your groups matter. A lot. The reality is that the people in groups, from a research vantage point, are more likely to share their faith, repent of sins regularly, give sacrificially, serve faithfully, and read their Bibles. And based on the research and based on our experiences with small groups (we both lead groups in the churches we serve), we can confidently encourage you to do these things as you elevate the priority of groups in your context. After a previous research project, the Transformational Discipleship project, I (Eric) wrote a book, entitled *Transformational Discipleship* along with Philip Nation and Michael Kelley. In the book we describe something known as the Transformational Sweet Spot (see graphic below). It's the intersection of three characteristics that we describe as truth, posture, and leader. We believe the intersection of these three key ingredients is where disciplemaking is most likely to occur. As we consider what is required for groups to be healthy, and to reproduce disciples, we are once again reminded of the Transformational Sweet Spot. Regardless of your group values (your manifesto), of your discipleship strategy, of the role your groups play in your discipleship strategy, and regardless of the types of leaders you assign to your groups, you must do these things.

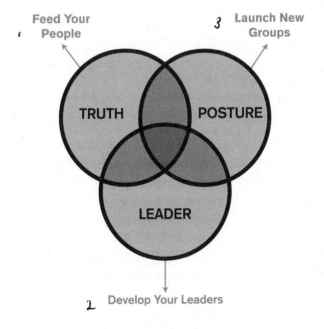

1. Leader: Develop Your Leaders

Healthy groups are led by healthy leaders. Your small group leaders will reproduce who they are. When the apostle Paul encouraged the believers in Philippi to put faith into practice, he did not merely tell them to put what they heard him teach into practice but also how they saw him live.

Do what you have learned and received and heard and seen in me, and the God of peace will be with you. (Phil. 4:9)

Whether you recruit leaders to be first teachers, to be first community builders, or to be first missional movement leaders, they must be trained and developed.

A holy cause and effect will take place if you commit to developing your leaders. When church leaders make the training of the saints their holy cause (Eph. 4:11–12), the holy effect is a more healthy body (Eph. 4:13). We have said it throughout the book, but take note: Your role as a church leader is not to do the ministry. It is ultimately to prepare other people to do ministry. And your group leaders are in a critical role to ensure the body is served and encouraged. You must develop your leaders.

2. Posture: Launch New Groups

The posture of your church must be that of launching new groups. Without new groups you will not be giving new people who come to your church a place to connect. Without new groups you will not be fostering a culture of reproduction. Without new groups your church will grow stagnant. New groups reveal a culture of reproduction. They reveal an intentionality to shepherd new people, a passion to gather people in community, and a strong conviction that people must be known and not merely come to a worship gathering.

I (Eric) still drive the '95 Nissan pickup truck my father and I purchased together my freshman year of college. The odometer reads seventy-seven thousand miles, but the odometer has been broken for well over a decade. The seats look pretty worn. There are scratches all over the side from my youth ministry days, hauling stages and equipment. I love my truck. There is a worn-down place on the driver's-side door where my elbow fits perfectly. Many great memories are connected to my truck, including my first date with Kaye and driving around practicing my first sermon. Another huge benefit is that it is hard to get a speeding ticket in my truck. The truck starts to shake violently if I hit seventy-five to eighty mph. It is a good check, kind of like a second Holy Spirit.

While folks verbally abuse my truck, it is not something I look forward to forsaking. I really don't feel like shopping for something else. I am comfortable with the same old, same old. Yet deep down I know that I will probably love the new vehicle I will one day purchase. A fresh smell, a less bumpy ride, a radio that works, and a heater that does not take ten minutes to kick into full gear will all be refreshing.

There is power in new.

In a local church there is certainly power in new. Though we wish this were not true, as it should not always be this way, the reality is that new has a disproportionate amount of impact. We have seen throughout our experiences and in research:

New small groups connect more people than existing groups. Once a group has been established, it feels closed. As a whole, new groups connect more unconnected people than groups that have been meeting for years.

New worship services grow faster than existing worship services. The energy required to launch a new service creates momentum and is often the place where new people will visit and connect.

New churches grow faster than older ones. Church multiplication allows for a new localized gathering of believers to impact a community and bring new people into the body of Christ.

New is powerful, but challenging a local church to launch new things can be, well, challenging. Just as I will struggle with parting ways with my truck, many people struggle with parting ways with the status quo. The status quo is comfortable; the new is unknown. The status quo is easy; the new requires work.

Yet for the sake of the expansion of His kingdom, we must launch new groups, services, and churches. Though the new is often risky and uncomfortable, it must be embraced.

We find it ironic that some churches talking about launching new campuses or new churches have not yet become skilled in launching new groups. Walk before you run! Become skilled in the art of launching new groups. There is power in new.

3. Truth: Feed the People

Jesus wants His sheep well fed. Regardless of the primary purpose of your groups (connection, mission, or formation), groups must be built on the Word of God.

In the hours leading up to His arrest, Jesus begged the Father for our unity. He prayed:

> I pray not only for these, but also for those who believe in
> Me through their message. May they all be one, as You,
> Father, are in Me and I am in You. May they also be one in
> Us, so the world may believe You sent Me. (John 17:20–21)

Jesus' prayer is a huge statement of what He wants for His followers. He desires for His people to be as unified as He and the Father, reflecting the character of God with our oneness. And because our unity reflects the nature of God, it is evangelistic. Earlier in John's Gospel, Jesus shared that all men would know we are His by the love we have for one another (John 13:35).

So, as we have been encouraging, wise ministry leaders preach and teach about the necessity of interdependent community with other believers. They work hard to cultivate a culture that values community. They strategize and put systems in place to move people to groups or classes. Deep down they want their people to be the church, not merely come to church. They know their church is only as strong as the groups in the church.

But as we long to foster healthy community, we must ask ourselves, "What are we uniting our people around?" As we build systems to attach people, what exactly are we attaching them to? The strength of a church's community will only be as solid as the strength of what the people are united around.

In the same prayer where Jesus pleaded with the Father for our unity, He also prayed for His disciples to be made holy: "Sanctify them by the truth; Your word is truth" (John 17:17). He wants us both unified and sanctified. Our oneness and our holiness are deeply related. When sin increases (gossip, pride, etc.), community suffers. As we are made holy, community deepens (love, patience, kindness, goodness, etc.).

And how are we made holy? "By the truth; Your word is truth."

As community built on the truth of God deepens, so does the holiness of those in the community. In other words, uniting people around the Scripture is essential for the health of our community. Scripture must define our community, and we must hold Scripture as the common ground for our unity. We must build community around the holy text that endures forever (1 Pet. 1:25), the living and active Word of God (Heb. 4:12), that is useful for teaching, rebuking, correcting, and training in righteousness, so that the man of God may be thoroughly equipped for every good work (2 Tim. 3:16–17).

Ministries that attach people to one another without some expression of biblical study are creating an attachment that is too weak—and a community too shallow.

Are your groups being built on the foundation of the Word of God?

One of the most disturbing findings in the research is that the majority of group leaders are not given direction or a plan on what to study as a group. Many pastors have no clue what their groups are studying. A wise pastor would never hand a microphone over to just anyone in a worship gathering to carry the burden of feeding the people. Yet every single week pastors and church leaders do just that.

We were so bothered by this finding that we conducted some additional research on group leaders. We wondered if group leaders like not having direction. Do they enjoy not being given a wise plan for discipling the people in their groups?

We found that 75 percent of group leaders say they want direction. Pastors, they want you to give them a wise plan of study. Groups are too important to haphazardly approach the study time. We must ensure our groups are built on a solid foundation. Feed the people well.

The Next 100 Days

At the time of this writing, a quick check showed us that almost twenty million new books were available on Amazon. You can check again now; we bet the number has grown. So, what will make this book any different? The difference will be found in what you decide to do now and over the next one hundred days. What measureable steps will you take?

When you go back to Ying Kai's story, God used a simple sign asking, "How many of My people will hear the gospel today?" to lead Ying Kai to new places beyond his imagination. Maybe God will use a simple book, or a phrase in the book, or maybe a story to start something new and big for Him.

We urge you to commit the next one hundred days to action. Make a plan of what you will do with what you have read. What actions will you take?

1. Begin with extended time with Him, a Bible, a blank journal, and one big question: "God, what do You want?" Make this appointment and refuse to move it.
2. Review the key steps in this book. Remember, we are not presenting them as a process so you also have the option to pick the steps that are most relevant to your world. Here are the steps:

   • Assess the transformational platforms in your church.

- Determine a church disciple-making strategy.
- Identify the appropriate style of group to support your church strategy.
- Discover and develop the right leaders.
- Create a transformational group manifesto.
- Define group practices.
- Multiply.
- Imagine the possibilities.

3. Continue the conversations with key leaders and leadership teams in your church. Don't force or enforce change. Speak to the head, then to the heart, then to the hand. Give them time to imagine new things for your church and community.

From the Group

What a relief it is and how freeing to live life honestly and openly with people who care about you. My walls are shorter and fewer than ever before in my life. I never used to share with anyone. Participating in a group has taught me the value of being genuinely open—with both the good and the bad. That's where real relationship happens.

—LIZA

What Now?

- Discover stories of transformation within your church and community. Celebrate them together as a reminder of what God has done in the past and what He wants to do in the future.

Notes

Chapter 2: Trees Don't Move the Wind

1. Brad House, *Community: Taking Your Small Group Off Life Support* (Wheaton, IL: Crossway, 2011), 19.
2. Brian's story is true. Throughout the book we use a number of stories, and each one is an actual story about actual people's lives and experiences in group life. However, we have changed the names of all those involved.
3. When we use the term "at least four times a month," there is generally a reference to those who attend a group weekly, but also includes those who may meet with an additional group at some other point during the week.
4. The phrase "positive response" means the respondent gave an answer that is expected of someone who is spiritually mature or maturing.
5. D. James Kennedy and Jerry Newcomb, *What If Jesus Had Never Been Born? The Positive Impact of Christianity in History* (Nashville: Thomas Nelson, 1994), 4.
6. Alister E. McGrath, *Mere Apologetics: How to Help Seekers and Skeptics Find Faith* (Grand Rapids: Baker Publishing Group, 2012), Kindle edition.

Chapter 3: A Discipleship Deficit

1. Andy Stanley and Bill Willits, *Creating Community* (Portland, OR: Multnomah Books, 2004).
2. Simon Sinek, *Start with Why: How Great Leaders Inspire Everyone to Take Action* (New York: Portfolio Penguin, 2009), 39.
3. Neal McGlohon, The Cypress Project, www.cypressproject.org.
4. Unless we say otherwise, you should assume that all our research of pastors is a multidenominational sample of Protestant pastors; and when we talk about church attenders, it's a multidenominational sample of Protestant churchgoers. Rather than list all the details, go to LifeWayResearch.com for all the particulars.
5. Dietrich Bonhoeffer, *Life Together* (New York: Harper & Row, 1954).
6. Joey Bonifacio, *The LEGO Principle: The Power of Connecting to God and One Another* (Lake Mary, FL: Charisma House, 2012), Kindle edition.

Chapter 4: Integration

1. *Integration* definition from http://dictionary.reference.com /browse/integration?s=t, accessed April 15, 2013.
2. Author-coined phrase found on blog; http://christianitytoday. com/edstetzer/2008/may/clergification.html.
3. *Clergy* definition from http://dictionary.reference.com/browse /Clergy?s=t, accessed April 15, 2013.
4. *Laity* definition from http://dictionary.reference.com/browse /laity?s=t, accessed April 15, 2013.

Chapter 5: The Right Leaders

1. Robert E. Logan, *From Followers to Leaders* (Saint Charles, IL: Churchsmart, 2008).
2. Phil Cooke; http://churchmarketingsucks.com/2010/11/phil-cooke-media-the-church.
3. Michael Gerber, *The E-Myth Revisited* (New York: HarperCollins, 2001).

Chapter 6: Group Practices

1. Joey Bonifacio, *The LEGO Principle: The Power of Connecting to God and One Another* (Lake Mary, FL: Charisma House, 2012), Kindle edition.
2. The Harvard study is part of a report published in the *Personality and Social Psychology Bulletin* by Todd Heatherton, a professor at Dartmouth, and Patricia Nichols, a professor at Harvard. See http://dartmouth.edu/~thlab/pubs/94_ Heatherton_Nichols_PSPB_20.pdf.
3. Brad House, *Community: Taking Your Small Group Off Life Support* (Wheaton, IL: Crossway, 2011), 106.
4. Tim Chester, *Meals with Jesus: Discovering Grace, Community and Mission around the Table* (Wheaton, IL: Crossway, 2011).
5. See http://churchillfellowsnsw.org.au/newsletters_3_ 1643228772.pdf.

Chapter 7: Multiply

1. Artie Davis, *Craveable: The Irresistible Jesus in Me* (Lake Mary, FL: Passio, 2013).
2. "The Cost of the Combine," http://blogs.nfl.com/2009/02/24 /the-cost-of-the-combine.
3. This is from a LifeWay product. This link is a brochure authored by David Francis explaining it. Their explanation of it is accurate: https://www.google.com/url?sa=t&rct=j&q=&esrc=s &source=web&cd=2&ved=0CDcQFjAB&url=http%3A%2F%2F www.christianitytoday.com%2Fassets%2F10034.pdf&ei=entMU sT4DJTeyQGN7YCwBA&usg=AFQjCNFY5qn60qpkI6W8hCA HMdmTkvcdrw&sig2=BLJw69w-9dNq99SCW1yHOQ&bvm=b v.53371865,d.aWc.

Chapter 8: Connect with Disconnected People

1. David Wells, "The Price of Modern Rootlessness," quoted by Ken Myers on Mars Hill Audio, *Anthologies, Number 3: Place, Community, and Memory* (Powhaten, VA: Berea Publications, 2000).
2. National Night Out, http://www.natw.org/national-night-out -registration.

Chapter 9: Imagine the Possibilities

1. Steve Smith with Ying Kai, *T4T: A Discipleship Re-Revolution* (WIGTake Resources, LLC. Kindle edition, 2011).
2. Ibid. Visit www.t4tonline.org to see more.

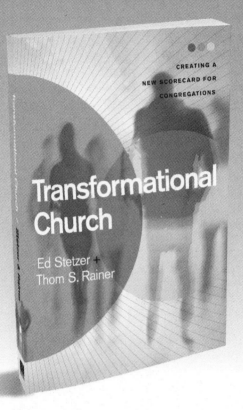

Also Available

Transformational Discipleship

how people really grow

ERIC GEIGER
MICHAEL KELLEY
PHILIP NATION

How People Really Grow

A broadly experienced trio of rising church leaders share substantive research on churches and individuals that will help readers foster a culture wherein people intentionally grow in their Christian faith.

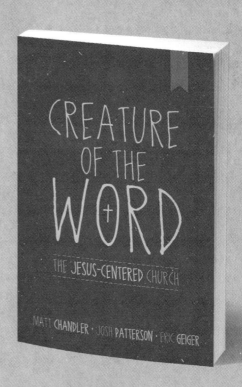

See Yourself, See Your Church, See Your World
DIFFERENTLY

SUBVERSIVE KINGDOM is a personal call for Christians to reorient their thinking and lifestyle to match what Jesus described of His people in Scripture, while teaming up with other believers through their churches to bring light into a dying and darkening culture.

ED STETZER is one of today's leading voices in helping the church stay anchored to its roots while becoming active in culture. He is president of LifeWay Research, as well as a nonstop author and teacher, a trendsetting church planter, and dad to three really fun daughters.

EdStetzer.com
@BHPub
@EdStetzer

SUBVERSIVE
LIVING AS AGENTS OF GOSPEL TRANSFORMATION

Ed Stetzer

AVAILABLE AT BOOK STORES NATIONWIDE

Every WORD Matters
BHPublishingGroup.com